BANK MANAGER AS TEAM LEADER

ANUJ SINHA

Ex Chief Manager (Regional & Zonal Planning,
Inspection & Audit Head, RBDM, CBO Head)
Bank of Baroda

INDIA • SINGAPORE • MALAYSIA

Notion Press

No.8, 3rd Cross Street,
CIT Colony, Mylapore,
Chennai, Tamil Nadu – 600004

First Published by Notion Press 2021
Copyright © Anuj Sinha 2021
All Rights Reserved.

ISBN 978-1-63633-680-0

This book has been published with all efforts taken to make the material error-free after the consent of the author. However, the author and the publisher do not assume and hereby disclaim any liability to any party for any loss, damage, or disruption caused by errors or omissions, whether such errors or omissions result from negligence, accident, or any other cause.

While every effort has been made to avoid any mistake or omission, this publication is being sold on the condition and understanding that neither the author nor the publishers or printers would be liable in any manner to any person by reason of any mistake or omission in this publication or for any action taken or omitted to be taken or advice rendered or accepted on the basis of this work. For any defect in printing or binding the publishers will be liable only to replace the defective copy by another copy of this work then available.

Dedicated to the fond memories of my parents and love and affection of family members who inspire me always to make the difficult path of success easy, enjoyable and meaningful.

CONTENTS

Preface 7

Foreword 11

1. Why Do We Need A Team Leader 13

2. How to Become a Good Team Leader 23

3. Team Building 30

4. Challenges of Bank Manager as Team Leader 41

5. Listening Skills of Team Leader 51

6. Performance Review Meeting 61

7. Human Relation Skills of Team Leader 68

8. Customer Focused Leadership 75

9. Workplace Conflict Management 86

10. Stress Management for Team Leader 98

11. The art of Positive Criticism 110

12. Banking Industry at the Digital Age 114

13. SWOT analysis 119

14. Success story from Ms. Lakshmi Anand,
    Chief Manager, Bank of Baroda,
    Thillai Nagar Branch, Trichy, India. 128

Book Review *131–137*

PREFACE

It has been my experience during the last thirty years of working in one of the leading banks of the country that many good officers are not enthusiastic to take the responsibility of Branch Head as they are not confident to come as per expectations of higher management. This lack of confidence is due to a kind of fear psychosis that full of odds this post may land them in endless troubles. Shortage of experienced staff, half hearted cooperation of higher management and hostile behaviour of customers are some of the genuine reasons which create fear and low morale among these officers. In such a time of crisis it is necessary to fill the sense of courage and interest in bank officers to come forward to accept the challenge and show the performance.

The only practical way to generate good confidence in these officers is to develop the personality traits of bank managers to perform as true business leaders which is the present day requirement of all banks. Every manager must be knowing what is expected of him at work. The job of bank manager is very challenging in the sense that if all the expectations of higher management are fulfilled without any extra efforts there was no need to place a manager. Looking to this most new generation bankers are hesitant to accept the responsibility of a branch manager. But once they develop their latent personality traits to face the adversaries, their confidence level is increased to perform as a successful bank manager. And for this a bank manager has to prove himself a leader of his team only then he can be successful in leadership position.

A team leader is the most important person for execution of corporate objectives by utilizing the available manpower. The role of team leader is one step ahead of managers in many ways viz. difference in relationship, difference in personality traits and their positive attitude towards achievement of goal. For excellent performance they must form a good team and focus their attention of casting of talent. Many bank managers just fail to use the available manpower resources judiciously and clamour for more staff forgetting the drain on productivity of the branch caused by over staffing or if the optimum utilization of staff is not kept in mind.

My intention behind writing this book has a definite and practical reason in sharing the concepts of leadership with a broader group of business leaders. To start with the basics, the necessity of having team leaders instead of bank managers, team building, listening skills of team leaders etc. have been discussed in detail. This book also throws light on how to develop customer focused leadership so that the bank managers can achieve the corporate goals through their customer centric approach.

I have written this book with the intention of helping the bank managers to prepare themselves for success in leadership role. Some of them might have witnessed how workplace conflicts distract the workforce from performance resulting in overall poor productivity. This book will also help them to learn to avoid or reduce the financial, emotional and reputational costs arising due to troublesome interpersonal behaviours and the art and science of stress management.

I shall be happy if my work in the form of this book helps officers to achieve their goal in the leadership role, to prove as successful business leaders and translate the corporate objectives in reality. Since my knowledge in this field is subject to updation with passage of time I shall welcome suggestions for incorporation in future editions.

FOREWORD

The importance of leadership role of bank manager is now universally accepted yet the development of essential personality traits in business leaders to prepare them for the challenging role of bank manager is most of the time overlooked.

The book "Bank Manager as Team Leader" covers the topics required for a bank manager to reach inside of his team members and release their talent into performance. For execution of corporate objectives team leaders are preferred instead of bank managers. The chapter "Why do we need a Team Leader" explains this in detail.

The premise of this book is quite exciting when you read the chapter "Challenges of Bank Manager as Team Leader". The role of bank manager is a transition from an individual contributor to a business leader and in this challenging role the bank manager has to face various challenges which have been explained in this chapter. Among these challenges the team leader is expected to devise his own strategies with all positivity in action and mind. Even then his strategies may not be fool-proof as far as bank's priorities are concerned. Therefore the bank manager has to make right strategies before hand and should form a good, vibrant and performing team. This has been elaborated by the author in the chapter "Team Building".

How a team leader can make the performance review meeting meaningful and what human relations are required from him along with the art of positive criticism are well written by the author of this book in a very simple but effective manner.

In any service organization customer focus is a continuous customer service approach which ensures customer loyalty towards organization. The chapter "Customer Focused Leadership" throws light on this important aspect. In today's banking workplace conflict and stress are very common and they distract the attention of team leader from achieving the corporate goals. If not dealt with properly they are likely to affect the overall performance, productivity and market reputation adversely. The initial symptoms and how to deal with this have been beautifully spelt out in the chapters "Workplace Conflict Management" and "Stress Management for Team Leaders". The language of this book is simple and direct. The contents are well chosen, very useful and excellent.

Finally if you picked up this inspiring book and are reading this, you are no doubt attracted to this subject matter. Thus you are already on your way to prepare yourself for the challenging role of team leader of your bank.

Best wishes and good luck.

From: Dr. Ajay Shrivastav (Noida)

Strategic Consultant – Organization Design & Development | Leadership Training | Professional Certified Coach (ICF)

Ex – VP HR, Tata Teleservices Ltd.

CHAPTER 1

WHY DO WE NEED A TEAM LEADER

Every business organisation has it's own objectives the attainment of which helps it in realisation of corporate vision.

These objectives are broadly divided into several segments of which the business targets are the most important. A detailed roadmap is prepared to achieve these business targets through involvement of all.

The business targets can be achieved both qualitatively and quantitatively only through improved sustainable and continuous performance.

In absence of this it is not possible for any business organization to make it's own space among it's competitors. Almost all organisations have come to conclusion that the functional teams within the organization only can dramatically improve their level of performance.

Banks are no exception to this. Earlier first line supervisors and employees used to feel isolated from the main stream and deeply frustrated as they felt that they didn't have their own say in the growth of business of bank and their contributions were not clearly visible.

When the performance of the bank was not up to mark, on a number of occasions they blamed hierarchy within the bank for poor and unsatisfactory growth. It was, therefore, felt that a team based organisation where group activity is encouraged and promoted can be a better choice to get the desired results.

And from here the concept of team leaders in bank came into existence.

The job role of a team leader is regular monitoring and qualitative and quantitative progress of the team vis – a – vis corporate objectives. For this the team leader has to motivate teammates and utilize their skills and expertise to formulate an effective performing team within the organization.

Team leaders are therefore, different from managers because they are entrepreneurial and forward positive thinking. They essentially have positive attitudes which make them different from conventional managers.

According to Scouller the purpose of team leader is to make sure there is leadership which is visible, to ensure that all four dimensions viz. Vision or goal, action and outcome, team spirit and attention to each member, motivation etc. are being properly addressed.

The main reasons why team leaders are needed instead of managers are as under:

A. Difference in relationship

Managers and team leaders both have to get the results in line with corporate objectives. While managers get work done by their staff and in this process most of the time they maintain certain distances from them; team leaders are empathetic towards teammates.

B. Goal Setting

Bank managers generally set goals to prioritize necessacities. So this is not a long term exercise in their mind. Team leaders set goals based on their personal wants and ambitions to reach the targets and in this sense they remain progressive. Managers tend to narrow the number of solutions but team leaders incorporate fresh solutions to any new problem. Managers see the work as something that can be done either through coercion or by reward and punishment. Team leaders have different outlook.

C. Difference in personality traits

Managers can lead the team up to certain limits only, whereas team leaders have their creativity, critical thinking and vision which help them to lead the team to much greater heights. Unlike managers, leaders are hard working, optimistic, positive, intelligent and analytical. Their vision to achieve the goal is distinctly clear. Such personality traits are generally missing in managers.

Responsibilities of Team Leader

1. To form a team with proper combination of skills, knowledge and expertise required to achieve the goal.
2. To make an effective strategy to reach the goal by involvement of all teammates.
3. To fix timeline, do monitoring and review the progress periodically.
4. To give feedback of progress and any hurdle in achievement to higher management.

Why team is necessary

1. Teams comprise of more people which means more ideas, **resources** and energy than an individual.
2. **Strengths and weaknesses are exposed in individuals** but in a team leader's **potentials are maximized** and weaknesses are minimized.

3. An individual's insight is not broad many times but a **team's approach provides multiple perspective to achieve the goal.**
4. Individuals share credit and blame alone but a **team shares credit for victories and the blame for losses.**
5. In a **team leaders are accountable for goal.** Individuals connected to no one can change the goal without any accountability.
6. **Teams can deliver more than individuals.**
7. **When people work as a team aimed at a common goal the task becomes easy to accomplish.** This is the greatest advantage of a team hence team is necessary.

Casting for Talent

A talent may be defined as a recurring pattern of behaviour, approach, thought or imagination that is available for application to get desired better results.

This pattern of behaviour must be used by the person in usual course of action to bring some productive and desired result.

We know everyone has some natural talent and the latent talent of a person is very important not his physical appearance.

Physical appearance of a person makes the first impression no doubt but the talent once recognized, has lasting effect and when applied appropriately brings amazing desired results. This talent may be thought, feeling, behaviour or even some skills.

Bank manager as team leader has to see beyond the physical to each person's latent true talents and utilize the same for achievement of pre set goals. He should not be pre occupied with the person's skills or knowledge or even educational background.

A team leader is required to position a person according to his/her talent i.e. he has to cast the person in the right role to get maximum of him.

According to conventional wisdom the pre requisites for excellence in any job of responsibility are knowledge, experience, intelligence and mental alertness. It is rightly said that knowledge is power, because it opens all the doors of success.

In order to develop professionalism, the team leader must acquire sound knowledge of products and services of his organisation. A person's exposure to different workplace in various capacities adds to his experience which makes a visible difference in his confidence and competence both.

Intelligence cultivated through good knowledge, high academic past records makes a person smart at work.

All these qualities can be developed in a person though over a period of time. But talent cannot be taught to a person overnight. Talents are like a driving force behind an individual's job performance. It is not that knowledge, experience and intelligence are unimportant.

It's just that an employee's full complement of talents – what drives the person, how he thinks, how he builds relationship- is more important.

In banks deployment of a person is generally done according to his/her past educational qualification and job related previous experience. Of course the need of the branch is kept in mind. A person with degree in marketing is generally put in marketing job.

Similarly people with IT background are placed in logistics or IT department which is logical and appropriate. However there are instances where people having experience of credit appraisal in administrative offices are posted as Branch Head of rural branch. In such instances the officer is sent to rural branch to complete his rural posting which is mandatory as per officers' service regulations.

Now let us have a look on the other side. A person with qualification of accountancy may not have inner liking and enough competence to do accountancy job, rather marketing of bank's new products may be his choice. Though this can't be generalised.

Still there are such instances which we have come across. So casting of talent becomes very challenging for the branch manager when he works as a team leader.

There is nothing wrong with including a person's knowledge, educational and social background on casting checklist. On the other hand it is quite possible that a person having IT background may have very good social connections. Being a local resident many influential persons may be knowing him and this can help him in getting new business for the bank.

He may be well connected to various government authorities occupying high positions. Many businessmen, doctors may be knowing him since long in that area. Here in this situation the person maybe utilized better in marketing or business development job.

His liasion with various government departments, doctors, teachers, traders etc. may bring sizeable deposits and other business through cross selling of bank's various products. If the team leader does not place the person's inner talent at the top of the list, he will run the risk of mediocre performance.

So what matters is what is inside the person not his physical appearance. Second, team leader should not be pre occupied with the person's skills or job knowledge. This is very important which the team leader must keep in mind while assigning a job to his teammate.

To get the better idea of a team member's inner talent, the team leader should talk with the person asking about strength, weaknesses, liking interest, aim dreams and of course future plan to realize the dream. SWOT analysis of the team member will be of great help in this regard.

In the beginning the team leader has to work with team member closely and explore his inner qualities and interest to cast the talent. However our experience shows that in banks this kind of approach is very rarely seen.

Except HRM personnel others are not cared as regards to their inherent abilities which carry utmost significance. A person thorough in credit appraisal and expert in loan documentation is put in branch banking which is primarily a generalist's job with focus on business development.

Those who like field job viz. pre sanction survey/inspection, post sanction follow up and recovery to check slippages are placed at the computers to do the routine job. A team leader has to break this practice and has to identify the person's choices, skills, experience and social connections as well to get the maximum output from him.

Even his family background is needed to be looked into. If the team member is comfortable at his family he can do excellent job in the bank. Further if the person likes his job role and is happy with his family he will try to put the best of his knowledge and skills and will also enjoy this otherwise he will just do what is asked from him.

A team leader is supposed to do for deriving optimum utilization of his team by casting each person's inner talent.

Again if a person has technical or some mathematical background he may be utilized in a different manner. His analytical aptitude and excellence will be beneficial for planning job or even for appraisal of credit proposals, of course after his grooming in this field.

In credit appraisal of large advances branches are wholly relying upon chartered accountants for obtaining CMA data even though there is a very friendly software available for this. Many times chartered accountants prepare CMA data to project a very rosy picture of the proposal as per choice of prospective borrower which are not realistic.

In banks many frauds have been detected in which wrong inputs were given by customer and chartered accountants which were not verified in the beginning at the time of appraisal. If the team member is given some kind of training in this field he will prove to be a good asset for the bank.

I know a bank manager, a post graduate in commerce who was very successful in his career and never failed to cross the business targets of his branch. In social activities he was very busy and was a known person to elite group of the area. He was also a Rotarian of the district and took keen interest in the activities of his club.

Some of his friends were holding good positions in government departments with whom he was in regular contact. Meeting people was his passion. Every month he used to meet government officials sometimes over a cup of tea or sometimes just to say 'Hello'.

He used to arrange doctor's camp, teacher's conclave, students' quiz competitions etc. So he was always in memory of these persons. Such connections helped him as meeting the business target of deposit, cross selling of bank's retail products, third party business etc. were never difficult for him.

Since marketing of bank's products was of his inner choice he used this skill in fetching more deposits for his bank.

Team leader must understand this. We have seen everyone has some talents – recurring pattern of thought, feeling and behaviour that can be applied to yield higher productivity. When we talk of performance casting becomes real challenge for a business leader because of following two reasons:

1. **Some leaders find it hard to see beyond the physical to each person's true talents.** Here what matters is inside the person, not physical prowess or appearance.
2. **Leaders are often preoccupied with the person's skills or knowledge.** People with marketing degree are inevitably cast into the marketing department and people with accounting background are siphoned off into the finance department. There is nothing wrong with including a person's skills and knowledge on the casting checklist. But if the talent of the person is not placed at the top of they list, the bank will always run the risk of mediocre performance.

Casting of talent is one of the unwritten secrets to the success of great team leaders. Some managers quickly split the team members into two distinct groups: "losers" and "achievers". They keep the "achievers" to clear the house of "losers" and place the "own people" to fill the gaps.

But best team leaders are more deliberate. They talk with each individual asking about strengths, weaknesses, likings, goals and dreams. They work closely with each employee and closely notice these things.

They take their time, because they know that the surest way to identify each person's talents is to watch his or her pattern of behaviour and actions over time. They add a third category: "movers". These are individuals who have shown some valuable talents but who, for whatever reason, are not in a position to use them.

In short, they are miscast. By repositioning each in a redesigned role, team leader will be able to focus on each person's strengths and turn talent into performance.

CHAPTER 2

HOW TO BECOME A GOOD TEAM LEADER

Every business organization has a set of proposed objectives which must be attained within the given time frame. This can be achieved through Bank Manager when he/she performs as a good team leader.

A team leader is the most important person in any business organization because the execution of corporate objectives is not possible without him. In a Bank the role of Bank manager and team leader are not the same.

The vision of business organization can be successfully attained through it's business leaders who work as team leaders within the organization. While bank managers have staff to work for them, team leaders have these people follow them towards attainment of corporate goals successful in a fixed time frame.

Here the team leader is responsible for guiding, motivating and developing his team and orienting his actions towards pre set goal.

The role of bank manager and team leader are different although both have the same objectives in discharge of their duties. i. e. attainment of corporate goals towards it's vision in a fixed time line.

According to Halelly Azulay founder and CEO of Talent Grow LLC, the main difference between leaders and managers is that leaders attract a following who have faith in their vision, while managers have people who do work for them without necessarily any particular vision in their mind.

Thus, managers are known for setting short terms goals, delegating tasks, resolving issues and enforcing policy. On the other hand leaders influence, command, motivate, inspire and lead the people i.e. team into action and attain the goal.

How to develop leadership talent

For a Bank manager leading a team for the first time is really very challenging. Practically when a manager is identified to lead a team by his controlling office, initially he is not fully prepared to accept the responsibility.

Many things come in his mind. Whether he will be able to cross the business targets of the branch and what support he will get from higher offices; these are the issues over which he is not sure. He tries to find out the quality of staff and whether he will be able to get the support of his staff?

Since many things come in his mind he becomes nervous. Further since he is not aware of his inherent personality traits which may help him in becoming a successful team leader, the responsibility of team leader appears him daunting.

I have seen many officers requesting their Regional Head not to post them as head of a branch. However, there are some tips which can help them in developing their leadership talents along the way.

These can be summarized as under:

1. Casting of vision by Team Leader

An important part of leadership involves casting vision. Some leaders forget to cast vision because they get caught up in managing. True leaders recognize a difference between leaders and managers.

Managers are maintainers, tending to rely on system and controls. Leaders are innovators and creators who rely on people. Creative ideas become reality when people are in a position to act catch the vision of their innovative leader.

An effective vision provides guidance. It gives proper direction to the team that cannot effectively result from rules and regulations, policy manuals or book of instructions. True direction for an organization comes from a clear vision of team leader.

When the teammates respond to vision of team leader following his guidance it becomes a reality.

2. Know your team

Before start of the journey you as a team leader take time to know your team members, their aptitude, skills, aspirations, potential strengths, weaknesses and ideas to reach goal of bank. Devote some time to listen them.

Have a friendly talk so that you can be in a position to get the maximum of your teammates in the conversation. After having a comprehensive idea of the team awareness on above points you will be able to formulate a leadership approach which leads to success.

By having a free and frank dialogue with the team respect and trust will also be established which is very essential to work together towards a common goal commitment.

3. Collective act of self awareness

In order to clear the air of emotional static the collective act of self awareness for a team leader is necessary. This helps in bringing up and exploring team members doing negative feelings.

For a team self awareness means tuning into the needs of members, surfacing issues and being intentional about setting norms that help. It is advisable for the team leader to make time for a daily "check in" at the start of a meeting to ask how each member of the team is doing.

The approach of team leader with empathy applies not just to sensitivity among teammates but also to understanding the view and suppressed feelings of others. He should create time and space to talk about what's on teammates mind.

This kind of system awareness is strongly linked to positive team performance which is the ultimate objective of a good team leader. Team leader can focus on both whom in the wider organization to help and where to get the resources and attention team needs to accomplish pre set goals.

Or it can mean learning what the concerns of others in the organization who can influence, directly or indirectly, team performance, or asking whether what the team is considering fits the larger strategy and goals of the outfit.

The team leader should exercise in group self awareness from time to time which will reflect in functioning of team. The exercise in group self awareness will allow frank and open feedback from with in which is very essential requirement for a team leader's success. This helps in boosting the team effectiveness, as it creates a positive atmosphere to work.

4. Spare time for your team

Your team may need your guidance and support every now and then. If you are not available to support your team in need, then the team may feel unprotected. If you are always tied up with your hands-on-tasks, you cannot support the team. Your team may look towards you for your support and guidance and you should be visible and available for this. Your non availability may discourage the team and they may lose their enthusiasm in between.

5. Uninterrupted communication with team

Bank manager in the role of team leader must possess the quality of an effective communicator. He should be able to explain the teammates everything from organizational goals to specific tasks. If people are not aware of your expectations they are likely to fall short so the team leader should be precise and specific in communication. There should be no place of ambiguity or confusion in his communication to the team. A team leader has to communicate on all levels: one to one, to the department and to the entire staff as well via phone, email and verbal exchange of ideas, information, development are the necessary ingredients of a good communication.

6. Trust and Transparency

For a good team leader trust is the most significant factor in building personal and professional relationship. Whether this is within staff of the bank or among clientele both are equally important. Trust acts as a glue that binds teammates and their leader together. When there is no trust between staff and team leader they may be acting in different directions though the goals are the same.

The result is very disastrous when they are working in divergent directions for the common goal. Trust is not only reliability but it should be seen in the larger perspective which implies trust is accountability, predictability and ofcourse reliability. When the teammates as followers of their team leader will believe in and trust their leader, they will see their role model in their team leader and will wish to be like him/her some day. It cannot be built up in a single day. It calls for consistency. Some of the ways a leader can betray trust include: not honouring promises, gossiping, suppressing vital information from teammates and being two – faced. These actions destroy the environment of trust necessary for the growth of business of the organization.

There is an old saying, "To err is human". Therefore it is quite necessary that those who work are likely to commit some mistakes. Team leaders are no exception to this. All leaders make mistakes knowingly or unknowingly. Successful leaders recognize their mistakes and accept the consequences without any reservation rather than trying to blame others. There are people who try to make someone else responsible for their actions or consequences. People don't want to reap the consequences of their actions if it goes against the laid down policy of bank. This is a very common feature seen in a bank nowadays. A team leader who is willing to take the responsibility of his actions and is honest and transparent with his team is someone they will admire, respect, trust and follow. That leader is also someone they can learn from.

7. Team leader should be accountable and responsible

Bank manager as a team leader should himself be accountable for his acts and be prepared to take the responsibility. If under his guidance there is no satisfactory progress and targets are not achieved he should be ready to take the responsibility willingly and for such poor performance he should not hold his team responsible and accountable. In the review meeting when the higher management points out the unsatisfactory performance of the branch team leader can't say that it was because of sub standard performance of his staff Mr. X. If he is asked to give the name specifically only then he should disclose the name of poor performer of his branch, otherwise he should take the entire responsibility upon his head. Since the team has worked under his guidance and supervision as per strategy, the failure and success of the team rests upon its leader. A team leader knows well how to use power and authority appropriately even then mistakes in day to day work particularly decision making at any level can never be completely ruled out. In such situation the bank manager as team leader must accept the responsibility which in turn will appreciate the importance of encouraging individuality.

Chapter 3

TEAM BUILDING

Some people think that a team is nothing but a group of people. According to them when some people just gather to form a group this is team. But this is not true. A team is quite different from a group of people in many respect.

When you visit a branch of bank you will find that a small crowd of people is within the banking hall. Most of them are customers of the bank. A few of them are sitting on the benches, others are standing in front of cashier's window. Some of them are waiting to be called for payment of cash or are keeping an eye on the digital display of their token number for cash payment at cashier's window. Then within the hall itself on another section staff and officers of the bank are sitting in an arranged manner and performing their duties. Sometimes they speak among themselves to help each other.

Now the question is: Which group of people of this banking hall may be called a team? Is it the group of people present in the banking hall or the staff sitting in an arranged manner on another side of hall performing their duties and even helping each other if required? The answer is very simple.

Let us first understand the characteristics of both groups. In the first group mostly of customers, they have come to bank with some specific purpose, deposit/withdrawal of cash, passbook updation, repayment of loan, seeking enquiry relating to some particular transaction, obtaining account statement etc.

Thus the purpose of customer as an individual is specific, as a group it is varying. In other words, the goal is not common to all members of this group. Secondly persons belonging to this group are not cooperating each other rather each one of them is doing just his/her own work. Thirdly there is no communication among themselves.

On the other hand staff and officers in the branch are cooperating one another. They have a definite task for the day and each one of them is contributing towards finishing of their work before end of the day. Very frequently Branch Manager of the branch also comes in the hall and does some work as if he is also a staff and not a Branch Manager. These qualities of the group of staff and officers i.e. common goal, communication, cooperation and collaboration make it different from group of customers present in the banking hall. And these are the basic ingredients of a team. When all these characteristics are present in a team it is said to be a good team.

4 Cs of a good team

As explained above a good team has following 4 Cs:
1. Common goal
2. Cooperation
3. Communication
4. Collaboration.

1. Common goal

When you go to ride a bus you first enquire about the route of the bus i.e where the bus is going. If the route of bus is towards your desired destination only then you ride the bus. So your journey is enjoyable and successful because at the end of the journey you reach your destination i.e goal. On the contrary if you do not know where the bus is going and ride it without enquiring it's route it is quite possible that the bus may be going to a place where you do not find your destination.

Similar is the case with a good team. Every team must set it's goal and all teammates must be working towards reaching this goal. This goal is common for all teammates. In a bank though there are different departments where the job role of each staff is different but their common aim is to surpass the business targets of the Branch by following the policy of the bank. The collective efforts of all teammates make the attainment of goal possible for the team. Further in a business organization say bank, this goal must be the same as fixed by the corporate office. The goal of different teammates can't be different as far as business targets are concerned. In a bank business targets are fixed and allotted to branch by corporate or controlling office and these targets are the ultimate goal of the branch.

Bank managers as team leaders generally set goals to prioritize necessities. If the goal of team is not known to teammates they will work in divergent directions and thus even working hard in absence of any pre fixed goal, they will fail to show performance. So goal setting is not a long time exercise in mind. Team leaders of good team set goals based upon their personal ambitions to reach the corporate objectives. Goal fixed by team leader is common to all teammates and thus the team performs as a good team.

2. Cooperation

One of the qualities of a good team is that it is cohesive. When the team works as a cohesive unit every member of the team will look out for one another. When a team member thinks of himself only and cares about no one, the team as a whole suffers. In a cricket team players work together and every one of the team thinks and cares for other. If someone is hurt all the players run towards him and extend immediate medical help which is required. Not only this if this team is lagging behind some score to win the match, all players of the team help each other to reach that score i.e. they play as a cohesive unit. This sense of cooperation amongst teammates make a good team. With this attitude of cooperation and partnership every member of the team contributes and in turn expects contribution from other teammates to make a good team.

There are a number of methods of developing this sense of cooperation among teammates. In a business organization especially banks this is the job role of marketing and planning departments to organise social events like get together, prize or award distribution ceremonies, felicitation to target achievers, launching of some new products etc. from time to time in which managers and their staff are invited to participate. By getting such business leaders together outside a work context a strong relationship is built which in turn develops a sense of cooperation among them.

3. Communication

A good team leader identifies what is important for his team and does not take much time to communicate the same to his teammates. Similarly the individual teammates communicate each other. Unless this is practised they can't build a good team.

A good and regular communication makes a team vibrant and productive. The teammates are always reminded of their sim in this way. This helps the team to move in the desired direction In absence of continuous and frequent communication it is quite possible that unknowingly they may work against each other. The communication of team leader to his teammates may be verbal or even non verbal. If the teammates are communicating among themselves, there is no confusion and the goal and strategy of the team is known to all and they are not duplicating work. By proper communication they are able to know the present position of team and accomplish the unfinished work to surpass the target.

4. Collaboration

Collaborative approach of a team leader creates transparency in the organization hence it is powerful. If the team leader is connected to his team and genuinely interested in collaborating with them they will think the team leader is thinking and vice versa. This collaboration leads to trust and the team supports vision of it's team leader. One way to improve collaboration in the team is to create some small projects and the team leader puts some other of the team as in – charge. The teammates work under his supervision and report directly to him. The team leader plays the role of a participant on the project instead of being a leader. When the team leader convinces teammates that he cares for them, respects their ideas, thinks on their suggestion and approach, this is collaboration approach. A good team must have this quality.

Be fair and kind

As a team leader you have to reinforce fair, honest, courteous and respectful treatment to others consistently. When you work as a Bank Manager you are required to be mindful of Jewish scholar **Hillel's** famous "**Golden Rule**". The Golden Rule will give you a model to follow when you are not confident about how to deal with people. Since you are working as team leader people are your most valuable asset whom you have to keep with you in your journey of achieving corporate goals. When you practise this in your behaviour you become stronger as all teammates are with you happily and willingly. You will get greater control over your behaviour which is essential to control your own actions and words. This Golden Rule principle is based upon the principle of mutual respect and trust, honest communication which makes your decision making fair and acceptable to all concerned. The crux of Golden Rule principle is **"treating others the way you would like to be treated."**

When you don't show your personal preference to a person or a group of persons in your team over another person or group of persons you are supposed to be fair. While making decisions you consider the merit of the case as well as what is right for your team and bank rather than what is right for you. Here in your mind the interest of bank is more important than your personal interest and liking. So you are guided by this feeling. Before making decisions you generally involve your teammates to get their feedback and points of view. It is not necessary that you are required to be dictated by the opinion of your teammates. You follow bank's policies, procedures and guidelines of your superior authorities. When you behave in this manner such actions on your part make you fair in the eyes of your staff and customers as well.

1. A successful team leader has good listening capacity and knows his teammates personally. If in discharge of duty he does something harmful or neglected for others which hurt their sentiments he apologises without loss of time with all humility. In conversation with teammates he shows all decency of language and is never biased

or abusive. Even when he finds that a particular team mate has been very casual in his work he controls his temper and shows no verbal or non verbal expression of anger. If he does not apply this in his own behaviour his teammates will sooner or later lose their confidence in him. In the beginning the teammates may react or counter the team leader but after some time they may stop speaking and may not cooperate. So there is a gap between the team leader and teammates due to wrong behaviour of team leader. This gap is very dangerous in the way of performance of the team. Not only this it is likely to hamper the conducive environment of the branch and there may be infighting among teammates as well on trivial matter. So team leader must be very cautious in dealing with his teammates.

2. For a doctor an empathetic conversation with a patient makes an emotional connection which goes a long way to bring happiness, hope and will to fight the disease till the patient is cured. On the contrary if the gesture and behaviour of doctor is not helpful or courteous the patient will always have some doubt that he will be cured without loss of much time. The patient must be hopeful that his treatment is in the hands of an able doctor so he shouldn't have any anxiety. This makes the task of doctor easy. And this is largely dependent upon listening capacity of doctor with empathy. Such empathetic behaviour of doctor with patient greatly increases diagnostic accuracy and enhances satisfaction and loyalty of patient.

Similar is the case with bank manager when he is a team leader. The behavioural empathy of bank manager makes his interaction with teammates or even customers more connected and live. Emotional empathy means we recognize what other person thinks and it is not necessarily the another form of sympathy. For a team leader empathetic concern is of vital significance.

Self Assessment for Team Leader related to being Fair, Tolerant, Kind and Honest

This is very useful exercise for a team leader of a bank for relating on his/her being fair, tolerant, kind and honest. For this self assessment test the personality trait/behaviour pattern/conduct can be rated on three point scale as under:

1. I do this always.
2. I use this skill occasionally.
3. I do not use this skill

A. Fairness

Demeanour/Conduct	Self Rating (1, 2 or 3)
I practice bank's rules,, policies and guidelines	
I do not favour a person or a group of persons over other person or a group of persons.	
My decisions are based upon bank's interest and they are impartial.	

(Contd.)

Demeanour/Conduct	Self Rating (1, 2 or 3)
My decisions are not unilateral. In making major decisions I usually Involve my teammates.	
In assigning any responsibility to my teammates, I consider their knowledge, experience, ability and interests.	
In nominations for training of my teammates, I never do favouritism.	
In resolving customer grievances or disputes, I take decisions based upon the merit of the case.	

B. Tolerance

Demeanour/Conduct	Self Rating (1, 2 or 3)
I am not aggressive or hostile towards view points/opinions of my teammates which are different to my view points.	
I value and respect view points different from my own.	
I allow my teammates to express their view points freely.	
I am not biased and listen to my teammates/customers happily.	
When any of my teammates fail to complete his/her assigned job, I try to understand his/her genuine difficulty and extend my support.	

C. Kindness

Demeanour/Conduct	Self Rating (1, 2 or 3)
I listen the problem of my staff sympathetically and try to help them as far as possible.	
When a customer approaches bank just after business hour for cash withdrawal but before closure of cash department I try to help the customer.	
I am sympathetic to any problem in the family of my staff.	
I arrange for extra additional support to my staff when he/she is overburdened due to large crowd of customers.	
I consider the leave request of my staff sympathetically on merit and do not reject the same rudely.	

D. Honesty

Demeanour/Conduct	Self Rating (1, 2 or 3)
I do not speak lies.	
People(staff and customers both)believe on my saying.	
I speak what I do.	
I give true feedback to my superiors.	
Even when confronted, I take the side of truth.	

(Contd.)

Demeanour/Conduct	Self Rating (1, 2 or 3)
I do not wage my words and actions from the angle of personal gains, rather defend the truth always.	
In order to avoid unpleasantness of having to speak the whole truth, I do not speak half truths.	

CHAPTER 4

CHALLENGES OF BANK MANAGER AS TEAM LEADER

The role of Bank Manager as Team Leader is nothing but a transition from an individual contributor of business organization to a leader who is expected to do the work and lead the team for realizing bank's corporate goals.

This transition for a first time manager is rather difficult as he faces many challenges in the role of team leader. The challenges have multi faceted dimension. The internal conflict of staff, non cooperation from higher management and also hostile approach of customer make the task of team leader very difficult. Unless Bank Manager understands these challenges he cannot make any workable strategy to overcome them.

Common challenges of a team leader

Most common challenges of a Bank Manager as Team Leader can be summarized as follows:

1. **Adjustment and coordination of people** – Bank Manager as a team leader has to adjust people in such a way that he is acceptable to all and gets respect. His staff are the most valuable asset through which he has to sail in the tidy waves and realize the dream of corporate office. He has to coordinate those also who are not in his direct line of authority.

2. **Managerial effectiveness** – The team leader has to develop his managerial and personal skills. Time management, stress management and leadership quality are such skills which a Bank Manager is required to develop to become good team leader.

   Though controlling office arranges some class room trainings on these personality development programmes from time to time, team leader is supposed to learn them and practice the learning in his day to day working.

3. **Inspiration and motivation** – For the staff of the branch team leader should be a source of inspiration. He should have a thorough knowledge of bank's various product and services and be capable to guide the staff when they are not able to go ahead. The team leader should motivate the staff to get optimum result.

4. **To overcome internal politics and conflicts** – The team leader is required to have a clear understanding of bank's corporate objectives and the areas in which his team is lagging. He has to keep his eyes and ears open to have a general idea of what is going in the branch among the staff. He should have courage to give his advice to superiors to improve the situation. Unless he gets a clear picture of corporate office structure, thinking, vision and policies he cannot get desired results and success.

5. **Leadership and guidance to team** – Team leader has to give proper guidance and support to his team and should lead them. Regular feedback, monitoring the progress and receiving correct information on his competitors in the market can him in making suitable strategy to achieve corporate objectives. Team leader is supposed to take this task as challenge.

6. **Review of performance** – The team leader should hold periodical review of his individual subordinates. Poor performance of the teammates must be discussed and the weak areas be found out. A suitable strategy should be drawn up. For lack of knowledge, skill, experience the subordinates must be held accountable and should be guided properly so that they can also contribute.

7. **Communication** – Team leader has to communicate at all levels in his own business organization, staff, other players in the same field in area of operation, government authorities etc. The communication should be meaningful and effective. What is expected from teammates the leader must communicate the ways and means including strategies and plan of action to achieve the goal. Written communication in this regard from time to time is always preferred.

8. **Conflict management** – It is in the interest of organization that the team leader identifies and addresses all issues, however small in the bank before they convert into larger conflict. The team should develop such skill to resolve any issue of conflict among the staff well in time. If it is not taken care timely it may be very disastrous and may cause a loss of reputation and business of the branch.

9. **Leading different type of people** – It is not necessary that all the staff given to a Bank Manager have the same skill and capability. While some are very hard working, positive in attitude, sincere and honest others may be lacking these qualities making the task of team leader more difficult to achieve. The team leader must possess the quality to adopt them for a common goal as perceived by the organization.

Make your own strategy

The word "strategy" comes from "battlefield" and it refers to the art of winning a battle by the commander. That means how you deploy your available resources to achieve the desired result.

In bank as a team leader you have to make your own strategy to be successful. For this first you have to get a clear idea where your branch is standing in terms of business because business growth is the most important criteria of success of any Bank.

You have to reorient your present business to a fresh in line with your goal. For this all kinds of human working tools are to be energised and new tactics by perceiving the novel position have to be focused upon. Once the strategies are drawn up action points must be communicated to team members. Your communication to team members must show determination and passion to achieve the set goal but it should never lack emotional empathy.

This is because unless there is emotional empathy your team may not work in a cohesive manner and their divergent approach and outlook may smartly fail your whole plan innocently.

You must be remembering the story of Arjun in Mahabharat known as Dronacharya's bird eye test. While everyone in this test set their eyes on everything like tree, leaves, branches, bird etc. Arjun had set his eyes on his goal i.e pupil of eye of bird. The tree, leaves, branches and bird posed distraction for him but he focused towards his goal with concentration.

That was his strategy on which he worked and got success. There are so many irrelevant things in your working environment which you have to ignore otherwise they will consume your energy to make you weak in performance. For excellent performance your determination and strong will power with focused strategy is essential.

Positivity in action and mind

Negativity in mind always focuses us on a narrow range which repeatedly upsets our plan of action. When this is allowed to continue this offers a recipe of depression. A man trapped in depression cannot have an optimistic approach in his behaviour and action and he cannot energise his teammates. This is basics of all cognitive behavioural therapy which encourages the mind to bring good feelings.

A positive attitude is contagious. A positive minded leader is the centre point of attraction for his entire team. If your team is led and surrounded by happy and positive people, they will work harder and be happier themselves. In your workplace positivity may have different forms which is reflected even in your outward email tone. You should do your best to create a positive supportive environment during the work day. And this should also continue in your external appearance as well, be it meeting with your superiors, any social gathering or meeting with government authorities.

Some leaders conduct strategy review meetings periodically and only focus on the problems.

You definitely want to be aware of the issues but that is not enough. You must take time to recognize things that are going well with your strategy and celebrate success. Periodical reviews are necessary but strategies are required to be changed or modified depending upon the situation. If the results are well in consonance with the desired goal extra energy and added team spirit is enough otherwise some modification in strategy will be needed.

You are not always right

In execution of your action plan you may not be always on the right path. Sometimes it happens that you started on the right track but due to some unexpected development the path is diverted. If you think that you are better than others is always dangerous but most dangerous of all is to appear to have no fault or weakness in you. In the face of a superior skill, talent or power you are likely to get yourself disturbed. This disturbance in your self image of superiority cannot last long without stirring up ugly and undesirable emotions within you. One of the strategies to deal with this kind of destructive emotions of envy within you is to understand that as you gain power of number one, those below you will feel envious of you. This is not visible but is inevitable. As a team leader you have to read silently between the lines of criticism, sarcastic remarks, the signs of backstabbing and also the excessive praise that is preparing you for a sudden fall. This is to be recognized without any loss of time. Team leader has to develop this kind of skill within him.

When you make a strategy to surpass your target not only in terms of numbers but also to occupy the top position in public image, some of your subordinates may silently put obstacles in your path that you will not foresee. To defend yourself against this type of attack is difficult but not impossible. In such a situation you should strategize to forestall it before it grows to lay you down.

Team Confidence

According to C. Gene Wilkes power of team work cannot be underestimated in the business world due to following reasons –

1. Team affords more resources, ideas, energy and enthusiasm of people.
2. Team is the best place to maximize leaders' potential and minimize the weaknesses.
3. Team is able to devise several alternatives for each situation and this process is ongoing.
4. In a team the credit for success and blame for failure is always shared which ushers in humility and authentic community.
5. Team keeps leaders accountable for goal.

When you win the confidence of your team you win over your ego, sense of insecurity. Also an introvert person can enjoy the benefits of being in a team.

As a leader you should create a positive leadership culture so that your team gives confidence in you to work together and deliver for the organization. To be successful as a team leader you should focus on your vision and the people you have. By vision we mean where you want to lead your team by executing the business plan of your corporate office. The goal or plan will be executed by the people who are your teammates. Your focus on these two will bring them closer and your task will be easy. If you ignore your people but focus on goal only you cannot get true involvement of your team for achievement of result. Once the result is achieved your humility comes to play vital role. You should give the credit of your success to your people which will again energise them making your difficult path comfortable and enjoyable for you.

As a team leader you have to take the initiative. Here your proactive approach is required. Sometimes the role of a Bank Manager is very challenging. You have to face this whether this relates to old system of doing the work, indifferent approach to customers' grievances, apathy to staff genuine demands and issues etc. As a team leader you have to break the myth. You will have to remove complacency from the mind of your teammates by your own example.

Once you have been chosen as a team leader think that in the eyes of your superiors you are the best choice for that assignment. So take this as an opportunity. But to reach the highest level of leadership you need to develop your team.

Characteristics of a good team

1. Team members clearly know the vision of bank and what is important for them.
2. There is no communication barrier between team members.
3. Team members are always ready to help each other.
4. Team members are ready to sacrifice their personal interests, ego and certain rights for betterment of the team.
5. Every team member is aware of current position of team where it stands.
6. Each team member is motivated enough to present him/her self as a role model for others.

As a team leader you should develop a strong team which has full dedication and commitment to work under you willingly.

Effective Communication Skills

Bank Manager in the role of Team Leader must possess the quality of an effective communicator. He should be able to explain his teammates everything from organizational goals to day to day specific task whether this is solving of customers' problem or reaching a higher level of performance on the ladder of success towards corporate objectives. For this the team leader has to communicate with his people effectively which is understandable to each of them. If people are aware of team leader's expectations they cannot fall short. Therefore team leader should be precise and specific in his communication. The communication should be direct though the team leader has to communicate at all levels. Here a steady flow of verbal and non-verbal exchange ideas, views and information makes a good communication. From time to time bank manager should make his team aware of bank's priorities through clear and effective communication.

Good communication is helpful for bank manager in casting his vision effectively and to get the response of the staff equally. As the American President Gerald Ford had said, "Nothing in life is more important than the ability to communicate effectively." Hence a good communication can never be one sided. To be it effective it has to be positive interaction between the team leader and his people. Good communication always focuses on the response of the person to whom team leader is talking. Sometimes in this process even reading of body language helps a lot. When the team leader is talking to his people he must eye contact to make his communication interesting, credible and worth listening.

Interaction with clients

Customer engagement for a bank cannot be achieved in a day, week or a month. It is based upon banker – customer relationship which starts with a dialogue, understanding each other's aspirations, proactive approach in helping each other, building of mutual trust, steady but positive growth in service ownership and a growth in share of wallet. According to Gallup research the realistic benefits of a fully engaged customer that is both loyal in attitude and attached by emotions. This results in

a. Increased revenue, product penetration
b. Increase in purchase intent and consideration of bank's products
c. Improvement in customer acquisition
d. Strong willingness to become a Financial Partner

A banker as a team leader should adopt a client oriented relationship and should not depend wholly upon automation system implemented in the organization. Relationship with bank's call centre, at many times is like an annoyance rather than appreciation for intended convenience for a client. When we compare an automated system offering a number of options, followed by pre recorded message, none of which are suitable for original query; a human voice is very much preferable. Hence a banker as a team leader cannot leave his client at the mercy of automated system.

A banker as a team leader should understand various types of customer interactions which are basically of four types namely general, predictable, unpredictable and unwanted interactions. At the same time team leader had to use the required behaviour with his clients namely greeting, understanding, agreeing, solving and closing the interaction. He has to develop in him the required skills of interaction with clients. During interaction it is expected from him to be empathetic showing sympathy and willingness to help the customers' genuine demands. He cannot have a negative argument rather should lead a positive deliberation, should be friendly and have patience to listen.

CHAPTER 5

LISTENING SKILLS OF TEAM LEADER

Hearing and Listening

The process of linguistic communication covers both sending and receiving of messages. Business leaders are good listeners due to their nature of job. However hearing and listening both are not the same. Both are different from each other.

A physiological process in which sound waves cause our eardrums vibrate is hearing. Listening is a step further. The vibration is carried to the inner ear and is translated into electrical impulses. This is again carried to the central auditory system of brain where these impulses are identified as sounds.

This process is very fast. Listening first involves paying close attention to the speech and then interpreting it. This listening is different from hearing.

How to improve listening ability

Listening ability of a person can be improved through the following methods –

1. Desire to learn – Listening can be improved by developing the desire to learn and listen. This is the basic requirement. The listener should first identify his shortcomings as a listener and then try to improve his listening capability.

2. Concentration on listening – The listener should concentrate on main points of speech. Evaluation of evidence in terms of its accuracy relevance and objectivity comes after that.
3. Removal of distractions – The listener shouldn't allow any kind of distraction physical or mental to take place during the process of listening. He should focus on the message of speaker only.
4. Taking time for evaluation – When the speaker hasn't finished the speech the listener should not jump to interrupt and make conclusions. Any kind of mental or emotional blocks should be removed. In order to be a good listener one has to keep his mind open to ideas and information given by the speaker in his speech.
5. Noting down of key words – The listener should note down the main points of message of speaker to elaborate the same when the speech is over. This is the easiest method of acquiring the crux of the speech. This will help the listener to keep track of speaker's main thrust in speech.

What is Listening

Listening is the process of receiving, constructing, meaning from and responding to spoken and/or nonverbal message with thoughtful attention. Thus listening means understanding and comprehending the message by applying own mind. Listening is different from hearing.

It is purposeful hearing through mind. This type of hearing is called active listening because it requires certain behaviour of the listener. Active listening helps in gaining information about what is happening in the organization.

Importance of Active Listening

For team leaders active listening skills are tools for extending far beyond academic and professional settings. Due to the following reasons active listening is essential for inculcating good practice communication in team leaders:

(a) Without effective and purposeful listening, communication is incomplete.

(b) A good listener is a better learner than an indifferent listener.

(c) Team leaders having the skills of active listening can detect prejudices and attitudes of the speaker.

Active listening is advantageous and hence important because:

(1) It helps in improving relationship

(2) It improves our level of knowledge

(3) It helps in understanding other's point of view.

(4) It prevents problems escalating

(5) It saves time and energy

(6) It can save money and can give better results.

(7) It increases productivity.

There was an article in Harward Business Review which categorised listening into following three categories:

A. **Internal Listening** – When we focused on our own feelings and interest and pretend to focus on others it is called internal listening.

B. **Focused Listening** – As name suggests when we focus on the message of speaker but are not really focussing our mind on the message heard this is called focused listening.

C. **360° Listening** – When we are listening with all awareness, attention of mind etc., this is 360 degree listening.

By engaging themselves in 360° listening team leaders can increase the productivity of organisation because in conversation they can understand well how listening skills can be used for better performance. The listening skills of a team leader require to be more present, attentive, open and flexible. In the present era of digitalization, due to ever increasing availability of information on internet and digital form, the art and skill of active listening are diminishing gradually.

According to Peter Drucker, "The most important thing in communication is hearing what is not said".

An active listening skill of a team leader has many advantages. It helps in building a good and everlasting relationship which is an essential trait of any successful business leader leading a team. Listening is necessary to have a true idea of a clientele's needs.

Unless the team leader knows the requirement of his clientele he can't deliver the desired services of his clientele. Till a few years ago Nokia, BlackBerry and Kodak had their lion shares in the mobile phones market but they suffered heavily as they failed to their clientele's wishes and requirements. A team leader has to encourage others to be open and honest without a negative consequence. When team members offer their ideas in the form of feedback or opinion which are true and honest they help their leader to get the correct picture of the situation prevailing and accordingly make or fine tune their strategy.

On the other hand when trust level between the team members and their leader goes down, due to whatsoever reason, employees tend to nod their heads and pretend to agree with the statement of team leader though they have something quite different in their minds.

This important and burning issues don't get brought down into the open. This is disastrous for the organisation. And when the employees have trust over their team leader the situation is just reverse.

So active listening skill has following advantages also:

(a) It improves employee morale as there is transparency

(b) It helps resolve inter personal conflict as nothing is hidden here

It opens the door to new ideas, thoughts and possibilities.

Types of listening

Broadly speaking listening is of following three types –

1. **Discriminative Listening**
2. **Comprehension Listening**
3. **Evaluative Listening**

1. **Discriminative Listenings** – In every language different sounds are required to express different words appropriately. A person who cannot hear the sounds of emotional variation in other person's voice is less likely to be able to discern those sounds. So difference between different sounds is identified. This is called discriminative listening. It helps the listener to differentiate between familiar and unfamiliar language.

2. **Comprehension Listening** – This type of listening comprehends the non verbal messages conveyed by the speaker by attaching the meaning to what is being listened to. By understanding the body language of speaker, the listener is able to get what the speaker actually means.
3. **Evaluative Listening** – When the listener evaluates the message received by analysing the same it is called evaluative listening.

    Some other types of listening are:

    A. **Critical Listening** – In this type of listening the listener analyses and evaluates the message received. Critical listening means to scrutinise the statement of speaker and to make decisions coming to some solution to problem or analysis of situation without any delay. People involved in business generally use this as they get the main point quickly and reach to some conclusion.

    B. **Biased Listening** – When the listener hears what he wants subconsciously this is called biased listening. This is in line with pre conceived opinion of listener.

    C. **Appreciative Listening** – When the listener avoids engaging in other communication and concentrates mainly on the sounds or notes of speaker this is called appreciative listening.

    Listening music, story or any other information of interest comes under this type of listening.

    D. **Sympathetic Listening** – When the listener tries to show that he understands what the speaker is saying, this is called sympathetic listening. This type of listening is common among close friends, family members and business partners.

E. Empathetic Listening – When the listener feels someone's pain and misery himself by listening this is called empathetic listening. In this case the listener gives advice but without being judgemental with the motive of helping the speaker through the situation.

Degrees of Active Listening

Active listening means keeping everything out of our mind but concentrating on what speaker or other person is saying and acknowledging the same. In this way the speaker has the feedback that the listener is understanding and valuing his saying. However it is not necessary that the listener is agreeing to the speaker. So active listening is a structured way of listening and then responding to others.

The following chart explains various degrees of active listening:

Repeating	Paraphrasing	Reflecting
Perceiving	Perceiving	Perceiving
Paying Attention	Paying Attention	Paying Attention
Remembering	Remembering	Remembering
Repeating the words of speaker without any change	Reasoning in mind	Reasoning in mind
	Expressing the message by using words similar to those of speaker	Expressing the message of own words.

Skills of Team Leader for Active Listening

The key active listening skills of team leader are the following:

1. Team leader has to improve his listening ability so that the speaker or other person understands that the listener has understood what he is saying. Once the speaker feels that

he has been understood he calms down and the situation is de-escalated. This helps in problem solving.
2. Team leaders should use their body language to convey the attention. This may be in the form of non verbal gestures, eye contact, nod or physical posture.
3. Team leaders should have self awareness to present their thoughts, position, ideas etc. very accurately.
4. What we hear can easily be distorted if we think of our own beliefs and become judgemental before the other person finishes his saying. Team leaders should avoid this. However they may paraphrase speaker's comments.
5. The speaker should be allowed to put his views first and the team leader should not interrupt in between because the interruption may break the flow of discussion and ultimately waste time by diverting the main point of discussion. Interruption with counter argument is never appreciated as it is more harmful to healthy discussion.
6. Team leaders shouldn't threaten or lose their poise. They should never be angry while listening and shouldn't take things personally.
7. Team leaders are expected to put their views, ideas or opinion in a respectful manner. They should not hurt the feelings and sentiments of speaker.

Ineffective Listening

The effort of listening becomes ineffective when it fails to meet the desired purpose of saying. When the intention of listener towards speaker is focused it is effective listening. A focused intention helps the listener to meet the desired purpose of speaker's saying. The following is the list of ineffective listening–

1. Inattentiveness – The listener may get distracted. He may start day dreaming.
2. Pseudo listening – When people are not listening and are thinking about something else in their minds this is called pseudo listening. This is a bad listening habit.
3. Focusing on delivery – Sometimes a person concentrates on how someone says something that he pays little attention to what he or she is actually saying.
4. Rehearsing – When the listener is thinking about his reply before the other person has finished he is not listening. This is called rehearsing.
5. Interrupting – When the listener doesn't wait for the speaker to complete what he is saying so that the complete meaning can be determined but interrupts often resulting in a break of chain of thoughts of the speaker and thus disturbing and spoiling the communication process.
6. A team leader shouldn't have the tendency to accept only that part of communication which is consistent with his assumptions and beliefs. According to Stephen R. Covey, a renowned American Educator, the listening habit of a team leader should not take place from his own frame of reference. When it is empathic listening it is from other's frame of reference.
7. The listener may just switch off listening when he finds the material difficult to comprehend.
8. The team leader should not over react to certain words of speaker.

9. Multi Tasking – Checking emails, reading messages during conversation or keeping busy to work through files on table while a team member drops in to voice a concern, are some examples of bad listening habits. These bad listening habits come under the category of multi tasking. Team leader should not allow this habit to develop.

CHAPTER 6

PERFORMANCE REVIEW MEETING

The performance of a branch is reviewed on periodical basis in which the achievement of the branch in respect of various business parameters against allotted targets are discussed with the Branch Head. This is called performance review meeting or sometimes branch managers' meeting. The performance review meeting goes well if the branch manager or team leader gets organized and collects all necessary information before the meeting takes place. We summarize below the things which are required to do the night before review meeting takes place so that the branch manager or team leader representing branch is put in a great position for a meaningful conversation with the reviewing authority and the performance highlights of the branch are duly recognised and appreciated.

1. Discuss about the business of the branch highlighting achievements in the areas in which targets were allotted to the branch.
2. Talk about the development of business in terms of quality and quantity both. Areas in which branch could not show the desired results, explain the constraints and efforts taken by branch.
3. Give feedback to your superior.
4. Discuss your future plan of action.
5. With permission of reviewing authority set new achievable goals.

6. Your communication should be clear and effective. It shouldn't be ambiguous.
7. Exhibit flexibility. Remain proactive and avoid any kind of office politics.
8. If necessary suggest new tools and support of manpower you need to do your job as per expectations.

In addition to this list of accomplishments you should also keep mistakes you made and weaknesses you want to strengthen. This should be in conformity with your branch and your SWOT analysis done from time to time. Note that you learned from your mistakes and how you implemented changes to avoid making the same ones again. Save any notes or emails thanking you for your good work or noting your accomplishments by your higher authority particularly the controlling head. Trying to sit down and write all this up a week before the review meeting can be daunting and you are likely to forget a lot of important details. You should also identify your responsibilities and then evaluate yourself. Summarise in writing your accomplishments during the review period. Take responsibility for performance that fell short. You should not blame others for short of any performance. Create an agenda for the meeting, if the same has not been provided by your controlling office before the commencement of your performance review meeting.

How to deal with an unfair performance review

Sometimes the performance review is lot worse than expected. Your real performance is not given due recognition and any of your subdued or negative performance is highlighted in the meeting. The reviewing authority is not prepared to listen your difficulty and goes on pointing out only the shortcomings of the branch. If you start discussing over poor quality of untrained staff, withdrawal of manpower by the higher office during the review period the reviewing authority fails to appreciate your difficulties. Such a situation is likely to sting and will leave you very much disappointed as you will think that your good efforts were not recognized and appreciated but a small thing of little importance was unnecessarily stretched to give you a shocking feeling and humiliate in presence of others. You may also feel that you are being personally attacked which is likely to demotivate you. But this kind of emotional response would not get you far and hence it is important to know that the feedback is not a personal attack upon you but a constructive criticism to improve your performance and skills required for the job.

In order to handle such situation following tips are suggested:

1. Take a pause

Generally in a performance review meeting we go with a happy mood thinking that our performance will be appreciated. We think of our positive performance including achievement of targets and mobilisation of fresh quality business both deposits and advances. Opening of new deposit account of government raises our hope of getting appreciation from the reviewing authority. But things become more worse when the good performance is not given due importance and any shortcoming or negative performance is discussed at length. This is repeated again and again and when the review meeting is not one to one, one gets humiliated and thinks that he was not heard properly. On receiving such negative comment your instinct may be to give your critic a peace of your mind. You may even get disappointed if you continue to think over the matter. In such situation it is better not to react but to sit back, take a pause and avoid saying anything you will later regret when you are feeling less emotional.

2. Put the facts in a calm manner

Many a time the reviewing authority speaks something against you which you do not agree as the same cannot be corroborated with facts. It is not necessary what the reviewing authority is saying that is supported by facts and documents. Sometimes out of anger or ego he may speak something which does not apply to you. You are blamed for no faults of yours. There might have been withdrawal of manpower from your branch causing a stagnant position in the growth of business for which you should not be blamed alone. You might have been given a set of poor or mediocre performers or even one or two fraudsters which has always been dragging your attention resulting in hampering your concentration over business growth. In such situation if the superior authority does not speak of these negatives but goes on lambasting you on slow growth of business or poor performance, which you don't necessarily agree with, it is advisable to keep calm, take notes and then steer the conversation back to facts. When the boss is getting heated up keep calm and do not add fuel to the fire as it will vitiate the cordial atmosphere of meeting.

3. Maintain dignity in a professional manner

In a performance review meeting whether it is a review of performance or performance appraisal you should always behave in a dignified professional manner. This will help you in winning the heart of your reviewer to make the things conducive. Shouting abuse or indulging in arguments never helps rather it goes against you. By creating a bad scene in front of others you may lose the sympathy of your superior who is reviewing your performance. If you continue to indulge in undignified manner he may reprimand you and issue a caution letter or suspend you, which could easily have been avoided by maintaining dignity in a professional manner. Violating the well accepted norms of decency you cannot get the things in your favour though they may be true. The issues of concern must be addressed to the point in a dignified and professional manner and in a calm and peaceful cordial environment.

4. Admit and learn from your mistakes

When your superior authority draws your attention towards a genuine mistake committed by you, admit the same and assure him that you will make the corrective change. May be your boss has pulled you aside a few times on your complacency or failure but you chose to ignore him and are actually surprised to find it noted in big, bold letters on your review note. So it is advised to admit the mistakes and learn to make the changes that are requested of you. Unnecessary arguments over your genuine mistakes will be of no help rather it will go against you and will be documented to land you in trouble on a subsequent date.

5. Disagree with politeness

It is not necessary that whatever your reviewing authority says on your branch performance you should nod your head in concurrence. If you are in disagreement on certain points raised by your boss or if the facts corroborated by him are factually incorrect, you may dispute the same with facts and figures but in a polite manner. By doing this you will be in a position to direct the conversation to your point and then the reviewing authority will not at all feel offending rather he will show his genuine interest to listen you. If you are just contradicting him on every issue, sometimes he may take it personally and due to some ego clash your view points may not be listened properly. However, when you put forward your points of disagreement in a polite manner, showing the respect to the chair it is listened and properly dealt with.

6. Suggest for growth and improvement

The threadbare discussion in the performance review meeting cannot go waste if participants try to make it beneficial for them. Your active participation in the review meeting will help you in drawing some growth and improvement plan for the branch you are heading as team leader. Based upon the resources and potential available in the area devise an improvement plan that will help you get back on track and become a stellar team leader. Take this as an opportunity to come up with your own ideas depending upon your area of operation, potential available, quality and experience of your workforce and competition among the peers. Consult your boss for his input and seek his guidance for increasing market share of your bank that shows you have used the initiative to analyse the areas of your lacking in performance.

7. Request for genuine help

After having discussed the performance of your branch at length, if you have come to the conclusion that the unpleasant performance review is in fact valid, it is better to seek guidance and help in the form of support from the superiors. You might be lacking in an area, say lagging behind your business targets by a huge gap and your boss excels in that quality, in such a situation take some time, sit with him and show how to organize your work so you are efficient throughout your working day. You may fix some date with the superior officer and get the appointment with senior government officials of the area and request the reviewing authority to make a visit there along with you for fetching fresh business.

Chapter 7

HUMAN RELATION SKILLS OF TEAM LEADER

Various researches in early years of nineteenth century have revealed that performance of an organization largely depends upon human relation skills of it's business leaders.

In this context the **Howthorne Effect** reminds us of the fact that if the employees are motivated by their superiors or higher management under whom they are working, they excel in showing good performance and they become more productive. This motivation comes from a number of methods adopted by the team leader. Bank managers as team leaders are no exception to this.

When the team leader treats the teammates as special and takes care of them, they get motivated and they feel energised to work for the bank in the best of their capabilities which results in higher level of performance. A sense of belongingness automatically develops in them.

They start taking personal interest to give good results for the bank. The team leader is not required to remind them for completion of assigned job within timeline given but the teammates themselves leave no stone unturned to maintain the time schedule fixed for completion of tasks.

Earlier the management had a very different view of their staff. They believed that by nature people do not like to work for the organization as per expectations and they were not honest in performance of their duties and therefore, their performance was never optimum. They didn't want to share any responsibility and were not mentally prepared to go an extra mile for organization's growth. Whether the organizabition performed well or not this was not their concern.

This was considered to be the root cause of low productivity, sluggish growth of business and non achievement of business targets. Hence to overcome this problem the management always had a suspicious look towards their staff and watched them always as there was lack of trust between management and staff.

Later on after a few years this thinking of management was changed and they departed from above micro management oriented style and adopted a more people friendly and empowering approach. This approach is based upon the assumption that if the people are having a personal sense of commitment to the aims of their organization, the actions will surely be directed towards growth of organization. This was against the earlier belief that people by nature do not want to share any responsibility and therefore control and punishment were the only measure to get work from them.

When Mr. S. S. Mundra took over Bank of Baroda as it's Chairman and Managing Director in 2011 the overall position of this great bank of the country was not very good. The growth of business and it's market share had a sluggish trend in the banking industry. Slippages and non performing assets were going out of control. People were losing hope of reviving the old glory of the bank and they were losing their interest in performance. In spite of all these odds, in his inaugural address to mammoth gathering of staff and officers in Ahmedabad within a week of joining the bank he announced that for him as head of this bank "Staff

First" would be his priority. Everybody knows that the growth of a bank largely depends upon it's customers satisfaction over products and services they receive and therefore they are the most valuable for the bank. If the service to the customers of bank is poor nothing can happen as far as growth of the bank is concerned. That's why it is also said that customer is king of the bank. And the service to customers depends upon approach of employees. If the employees are motivated they will deliver the best kind of service to keep the customers always happy and satisfied. So by motivating the employees Mr. S. S. Mundra won hearts of the workforce and was very successful in showing exemplary performance of the bank during his full term. He introduced a number of staff welfare measures which were kept pending over years. These extrinsic measures adopted by him resulted in higher level of motivation and sense of belongingness among the workforce, increased their loyalty to bank and finally led the bank to a very respectable position among the peers in spite of stiff competition.

In this context **"The People Principle"** propounded by **Mr. Ron Willingham,** Chairman of Integrity Systems, a management consulting firm is very relevant and hence worth mentioning according to which if the unrecognized potential of people are tapped and accessed this can lead to far greater level of productivity which is beyond our imagination. And from this point of view in any organization people are more important than processes. In order to cut costs and improve productivity banks are nowadays deploying bare minimum workforce in branches. One person is now required to perform many responsibilities. Earlier cashiers in bank were always occupied with the dealing of cash receipts and payment. But now they are also doing ledger posting, though with certain cap, and cash receipts and payments in normal course of business in a branch. In such situation it is the responsibility of team leader to compensate the lost manpower through optimum utilization of available manpower resources which is possible only through developing the potential of workforce.

In the present environment the team leader is expected to change his outlook from old stubborn approach and thinking to new clear, logical and transparent one. If he thinks that the only reward he can give is a pay check, he can't get the desired success. It is expected from him that he thinks beyond this. Salary and compensation are important for which employees work. But this is not everything. It is the responsibility of team leader to develop his teammates to transform their lives as well. For this he must have faith and trust in them and through his support and encouragement he has to achieve bank's desired results.

Late sitting in Banks

In recent years late sitting in banks has become an usual practice particularly in urban semi urban branches and administrative offices. For some this is a compulsion or requirement and for others this is a problem with no solution. A team leader has to distinguish between the two. New generation bankers are energetic, focused towards their routine job and quite competent to finish their task within given time schedule. Successful team leaders are always comfortable with inter personal relations of their teammates and do not insist for late sitting unnecessarily.

A close examination of such late sitting practice prevalent in banks shows that in most of the situations this leads to decrease in efficiency of workforce and increase in bank's cost. Therefore unless it is warranted late sitting should be avoided. If all the staff are motivated to finish their allotted work as per time schedule, they will work as a team in cohesion, cooperate each other and at the end of the day will derive immense satisfaction. Also they will be in a position to take proper care of their family.

So feeling comfortable at home they will have a positive mindset and approach towards bank. Customers will also experience satisfaction and will be delighted to see their work done in time. For completion of their work they will no more be required to remind the staff time and again. Team leader should never be tyrannical or abusive towards his teammates.

He should find that if the employee regularly over stays after scheduled office hours, he is unable to manage time and complete assigned job within given time frame. Alternatively if some urgent job needs to be attended on priority, over staying/ late sitting may be allowed. Team leader has to ensure that his teammates are able to maintain work life balance and enjoy personal life with their families. When they return from the bank late in the evening they are not in a position to take proper care of their family which results in a tense environment and may be a cause of ill health of the staff. On the other hand if they return from the bank on time this will create a stress free environment in bank and the employees will be able to contribute more.

Team leader has to understand that people who are habitual of late sitting just to please their boss do not make any remarkable contribution in increasing the productivity, clearing the backlog of work, mobilising new business from area of operation and taking initiative to solve operational problems. Mr. N. R. Narayan Murthy, world renowned industrialist and founder of Infosys, also opined that people who regularly sit late in the office don't know to manage their time.

Evil effects of late sitting

Some specialised jobs or assignments that cannot be otherwise taken up and completed within regular office hours, may require late sitting in banks because such jobs call for undisturbed total concentration and uninterrupted special types of skills. In our early years of career when banks were not working on CBS platform, we used to do balancing and reconciliation of books of accounts manually which was very tedious as well as time consuming job particularly in big branches. Also during half yearly/annual closing of books due to tremendous work load and inflow of customers it was not possible to complete the job within scheduled time frame. And for that reason we had to sit late evening in the branch to complete the task. But whoever intends and likes to sit late in the evening does so, only with the intention of pleasing his boss also loses interest in sitting late after some time. These people fail to make any significant contribution to the bank. Not only this people also commit a lot of mistakes after doing hectic work for eight continuous hours which has been the universally accepted time limit for a man day.

The following is the list of evil effects of late sitting in bank:

1. People will pretend to work in late hours but in reality **they will be wasting their time and precious resources of the bank.**
2. **Employees develop a tendency to complete the routine job in extended hours** which they are capable of doing in scheduled hours of working.
3. **The enhanced physical strain and psychological stress will distort the work- life balance of staff.** They become disgruntled and quarrelsome.

4. The employees who are sensitive, **will lose their self confidence** and it will badly hurt their ego and pride.
5. **Late sitting in bank deprives a person of sleep for minimum hours every day.**
6. **It makes people very rigid and their behaviour changes gradually** from good to bad and bad to worse.
7. **It increases complacency** and decreases efficiency of staff.
8. Working beyond scheduled hours regularly deprives the new generation bankers of employment opportunities as they start leading life in a very unsystematic manner.
9. **Increases cost of bank** with no commensurate gain in productivity.
10. There is a danger of being branded "slow, lazy, inefficient and unproductive employee" by the management which is **likely to affect their career progression.**
11. **It has also been found that during late hours conspiracies are hatched, rumour mills are active, vilification campaign is at it's best, misinformation and canards are spread and frauds and malpractices are perpetraded.**

CHAPTER 8

CUSTOMER FOCUSED LEADERSHIP

In any service organization including banks customer focus is a continuous customer service approach which ensures customer loyalty towards organization. In customer focused leadership organization people, product, process and services are customer aligned. A team leader working as a business leader of a bank can't underestimate the necessity and importance of customer focused leadership.

In the center of bank's product and services, system and procedures, work force and team leader lies the customer. So everything revolves around customer as shown below in the diagram.

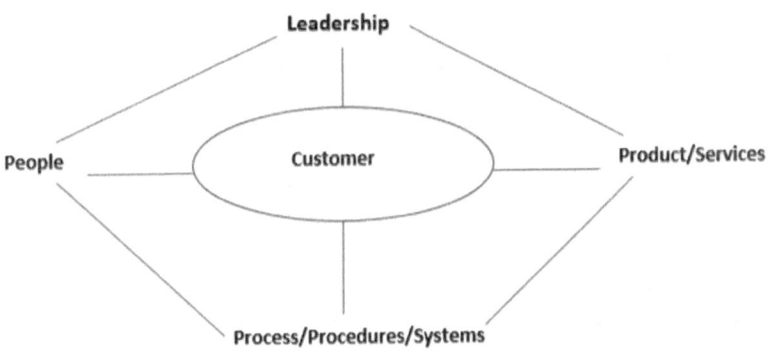

Therefore customer centric environment requires a customer focused leadership as a long term business strategy to ensure regular profit which is the crux of all business operations of any commercial organization.

A customer focused leadership ensures in the end, profitability which is very essential for the organization. If the organization fails to generate profit it can't survive. The main differentiator in the customer focused leadership is customer contact and support employees. Team leaders are supposed to create a conducive environment in which employees are motivated to render excellent customer service and keep the customers satisfied always.

In banks it has been found that mostly staff/employees treat the customers as if they are burden upon them. They forget that the business of bank is due to these customers whom they treat indifferently. They just want to dispose them off their queries without quenching their thirst of multiple questions related to their genuine needs. There may be various reasons of such indifferent attitude of staff towards their customers. Shortage of staff, excess of workload, non – cooperation from customers as well as staff are some of the common reasons which create an unhappy environment at counters of the bank. Though the queries of customers are answered at the counters but they lack human and friendly response and most of the time they are not as the customers expected. This causes customer dissatisfaction and if this becomes a routine affair, customer complaints arise. When such customer complaints are escalated they are resolved at the intervention of higher management but many a times good customers either suffer in silence or move away from the bank. This is a very painful situation for the bank as business of bank is driven away to some other bank which puts a drain on its profitability. This is never desirable.

Ingredients of Customer Focused Leadership

The key role of team leader or business leader of a bank is to ensure excellent customer service all the time. The most ingredients of customer focused leadership which a team leader must keep in mind are the following:

1. Customer centric actions of team leader
2. Regular dialogue with customers
3. Fast resolution of customers complaints
4. Fixing the accountability
5. Change of obsolete system and procedures
6. Reward and recognition.

1. Customer centric actions of team leader

The mindset of staff of a bank can be broadly divided into two categories namely Responsive Up Mindset and Service Mindset. In Responsive up mindset of bank the team leader communicates bank's goal, priority, vision etc. to officers/department heads which are executed by the front line staff who are responsive to higher management through their team leader. On the other hand in service mind set structure the situation is just reverse. Here the team leader views himself as serving the needs of customers. These two types of organization structure are shown below in the diagram.

78 ■ Bank Manager as Team Leader

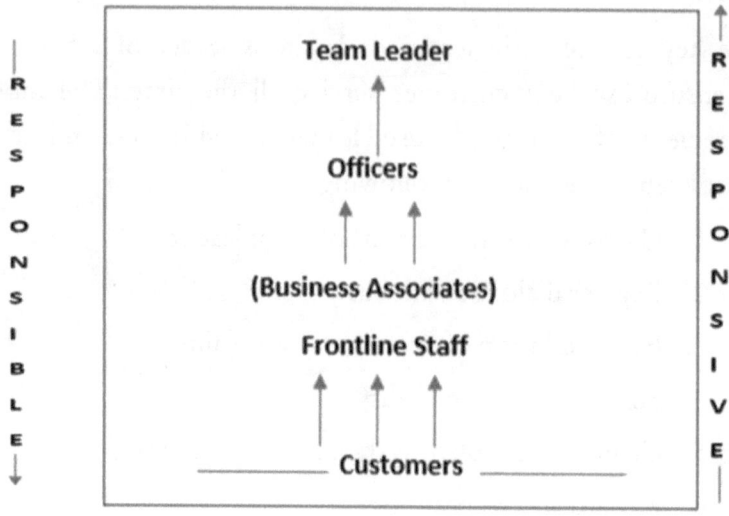

Responsive up Mind Set structure

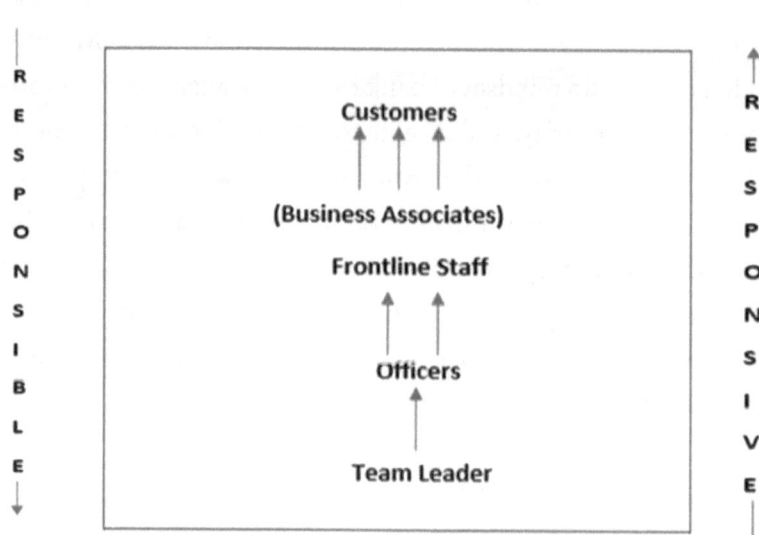

Service Mind Set Structure

In responsive up mindset of the bank the team leader communicates bank's goal, priority, vision etc. to officers/department heads which are executed by the front line staff who are responsive to higher management/team leader. On the other hand in service mind set structure of organisation the situation is just reverse. Here the team leader views himself as serving the needs of officers/department heads who service the needs of front line staff and who in turn service the needs of customers. When the above two are merged the leadership becomes customer centric. Here the entire focus is on customer needs.

2. Regular dialogue with customers

Regular dialogue with customers regarding their feelings, experience, perceptions and opinion about bank and prompt remedial actions on the same is necessary in a customer focused leadership of a bank manager. General customers do not express their grievances and expectations to the Branch Head. When they are not getting satisfactory service even after reminder, they remain silent and after sometime if the problem persists they leave the bank and the business is taken over by other bank in competition. Team leader must devise a method to receive the feedback and customer's reactions on bank's product and services from time to time and make necessary improvements to enhance customer satisfaction. Customer satisfaction is the most essential requirement of a customer focused leadership which every team leader must understand. Customer satisfaction on operational efficacy and staff behavior need to be analyzed and suitable steps to be taken without loss of time. Regarding suitability and modification in bank's product the matter should be escalated to higher offices with due recommendation.

Periodical customer meetings should be conducted in which officers/department heads should also be present. This should not be conducted in a ritual manner. In many such meetings customers who are vocal and wish to give their suggestion, they are not invited. This is a wrong practice. Minutes of the meeting should be sent to controlling office and necessary action should be initiated to improve customer service.

3. Fast Resolution of Customer Complaints

It is quite natural that every time all the customers of bank are not fully satisfied with the service they are getting. Sometimes due to excess work pressure on staff, time constraint or even the attitudinal/behavioural nature of staff customers feel disheartened. When there is some deficiency in the service customers are not satisfied and sometimes even annoyed to see that their grievances are not properly addressed by staff, some of them lodge complaints to Branch Head or controlling office. Survey shows that vast majority of customers do not complain about poor and unsatisfactory service instead they prefer to leave the bank. Though this decision is taken by the customers when they are repeatedly harassed and their genuine grievance is not resolved or nobody is there to listen them. This is a very painful situation for a customer because after having such a long relationship with bank now he is compelled to exit the bank. When this comes to the knowledge of the Branch Head it is very late as by that time the disgruntled customer is already approached by some other bank. Sometimes the other bank also offers such customer some preferential interest rate or concession just to grab the business. To mitigate this problem team leader should have regular contact with customers soliciting their feedback regarding service of the bank and if the customer feels unsatisfied die to poor response of staff, he should work with the teammates and plan recovery strategies for handling such situation before it is too late.

4. Fixing the accountability

Let us first understand the true meaning of accountability. Accountability is not fear nor a reprimand. Accountability in any organization is not simply taking the blame when something goes in a wrong direction. At the same time it is not a confession. Accountability is about delivering on a commitment. It's taking initiative with well thought, goal oriented strategic follow through.

Every staff knows that the quality of his/her service in satisfying the needs of customers is always in attention of team leader. At the same time team leader has to give right and timely feedback to controlling office regarding quality of performance of the staff on periodical basis. If the staff understands that he/she will be provided with fair and constructive feedback there will be more attention on their part in providing quality service to the customers. And if they are held accountable for the quality and standard of their performance they will endeavor to put their best honestly.

The word feedback has got immense importance in official work domain. Whatever information you get regarding a person from some other is feedback. A team leader is expected to get feedback on the teammates regularly. Depending upon this he may guide, encourage, support and mentor the teammates. Sometimes feedbacks are not correct. Team leader has to be vigil on this otherwise the very purpose of use of feedback will be defeated. Action taken by team leader on the basis of wrong feedback without verifying the true facts is always disastrous. Every team leader must know this. True feedback will help the team leader in motivating and supporting the teammates.

Team leader must put in force such accountability followed by suitable action otherwise a customer centric approach of staff can't be in practice and when the individual's performance lacks quality team leader's leadership is not credible in the eyes of the customers. For this the team leader must connect with team members. He has to make sure that the employees feel seen and heard by others on the team. This will make them feel like others are interested in their success, help them understand how their work affects others and increase their sense of accountability to the team.

5. Change of obsolete system and procedures

Team leaders are placed at Branch to augment quality business by executing bank's policies under the guidance and supervision of their higher management. In order to achieve this many processes are put in practice to ensure regular and uninterrupted workflow. Bank Manager as a team leader must be in habit of examining all such systems and practices which are helpful in increasing the customer focused environment at the work place. If it is found that some system is obsolete it should be changed without compromising on the quality of work and policy of the bank. No system and practice is good for all the time. Depending upon the needs of the customers they require suitable modification from time to time for whish team leader has to pay his due attention and be decisive. Many a time old system and practices become obsolete and their compliance and implementation is just cumbersome hence require change to ensure excellence in customer service.

6. Reward and recognition

Team leader must recognize and reward the employees who go extra mile to create an environment of excellent customer service. This is essential to boost up the morale of good and efficient staff. There are many ways to reward the employees whose actions show that they were committed to a customer focused environment. Anything from public praise in the work place (wall of fame) to a mention in the bank's newsletter or periodical in house magazine, gift card, lunch are some of the great ways to show employees that they are noticed and appreciated. The positive changes in the service performance of staff must be recognized and rewarded suitably. Team leader must ensure that employees know what they need to do to earn a reward. Of late some organizations have started to place photograph with name of good performer as ' employee of the month'. Even in many banks this is being followed and such performers are facilitated by their team leaders from time to time. This not only motivates the staff concerned but also sends a strong feeling among others that if they go extra mile to achieve something higher they will be duly recognized by the management and thus an environment of competition is created. This positive change is necessary to reach the higher goals.

I remember whenever I received any appreciation or trophy in my role as Branch Head from higher management I called an informal get together meeting of my staff and announced that the reward belonged to them because their collective efforts as a team had shown the result and I just represented them. This made my staff highly motivated as they felt their contributions were recognized. If this practice is not followed by the business leader the staff may think that their leader is being applauded for good performance which was brought by the entire team as a whole but the team is not getting any recognition and appreciation which they genuinely deserved. The good performance is the outcome of collective efforts of entire team of staff towards attainment of corporate goals although it is under guidance and supervision of team leader. Hence the contribution of team can't be forgotten nor it can be underestimated. This point is to be kept in mind by the team leader so that the team gets motivated and the task of team leader is made easy.

Summary

To sum up team leader is required to know the following –

A. What is the meaning of customer focused leadership and why it provides a competitive advantage.

B. To ensure customer focus what steps should be taken to demonstrate commitment.

C. How to develop quick and proactive recovery strategies.

D. What are the ways and means to develop a customer friendly system and procedure.

E. How to build a strong and cohesive internal service organization involving entire workforce.

F. How to get the right feedback from customers and how to proceed further.

G. How to identify and define customer focused performance standard.

H. How to fix accountability to hold people responsible.

I. How to reinforce a customer focused vision, values and standards.

J. How to measure and recognize customer focused performance excellence.

Team leader should develop a personal action plan for implementation.

CHAPTER 9

WORKPLACE CONFLICT MANAGEMENT

When there is a disagreement between individuals this may lead to conflict. When they are in a family or in an organization, conflict is inevitable over some disagreement. In management conflict arises due to various reasons, most importantly because of difference of views or opinions on a subject and inability of concerned persons to find a convergent view which is acceptable to all. In practical situation both the individuals think that they are right on their views and hence why they should agree with other's point of view. When both fail to reconcile, conflict arises.

The meaning of conflict in a work place can be understood in a very simple way by the following example:

In a bank branch, M/s XYZ is enjoying a credit facility of Rs. 10/- lakhs in the form of cash credit. As per term and conditions of cash credit if this facility is given against hypothecation of stock the customer is required to submit stock statements to the bank every fortnight/month and this is verified by the bank official bimonthly by making visit to party's godown. Based upon availability of stock the drawing power of the firm is worked out keeping in mind the margin fixed. Now if the borrower is not regular in submission of stock statement to the bank at stipulated interval, a penal interest is to be charged in borrower's cash credit account. Further if the borrower does not improve the position of stock and submission of stock statement despite bank's follow up the bank may view it seriously and ultimately if it is found on physical inspection that there is no sufficient stock at the godown of the borrower, details of book debts furnished by borrower are of very old period or not convincing to the bank, the cash credit limit of the borrower may be cancelled by the bank after giving proper notice to the borrower.

Now this is a very common situation in a bank branch. The credit officer informs the branch manager and suggests to stop debit transactions in the cash credit account. The credit officer may also insist to start the recovery measures against the borrower as per bank's guidelines. But the branch manager disagrees and asks the credit officer to allow borrower some time so that he may improve the position of account. Again even after this the position of account remains more or less same as there is no satisfactory progress. Book debts are not realized and the position of stock is also not very satisfactory. The borrower approaches the branch manager and assures to improve the position. The branch manager after listening the difficulties of borrower, agrees but the credit officer is not in favour of giving any time to the borrower.

Here we observe that there is a difference of opinion between the credit officer and the branch manager. Both are knowing well the full facts and are having their own points of view which are not the same. Credit officer is following the rule of bank as far as terms and conditions of sanction of cash credit (hypothecation) facility to borrower are concerned. When there is depletion of stock, money is not routed through the account because it has stuck in the market, credit entries are coming down gradually, interest is being served with much difficulty after many follow ups the opinion of credit officer to restrict the credit limit of borrower is justified as per bank's rule. At the same time branch manager's assertion to give some time to borrower to improve the position of cash credit account by recovering pending book debts from customers is based upon the risk of not losing the existing business of considerable limit. So from this angle, though there is always an element of inherent risk of not losing the business, the decision of branch manager to allow borrower some time cannot be held completely wrong. In order to retain business one has to take this kind of risk whenever required. Yes the past track record of the customer has to be looked into. Now this kind of difference of opinion between credit officer and branch manager is likely to lead to conflict.

This kind of conflict is defined as a clash between individuals arisen out of difference in opinions, based upon their perception and understanding. In above example we see that both the credit officer and branch manager have common goal to save bank's interest but their approach guided by opinions are poles apart. So conflict leads to war on paper, loss of peace of mind and sometimes finally in heated arguments if not resolved in time.

Common signs of team conflict in bank

When a new team starts functioning in a bank branch, in the beginning, the scenario is changed. All the staff are energised, have enthusiasm and the entire environment gets positive energy. The look of the branch gives a festive look. All the staff work sincerely cooperating each other. As a result after some time improvement in the working of branch is visible and customers are happy. The performance figures of the branch which had become stagnant, now start showing upward movement. But many a times this trend gets a sudden brake and the environment of the branch seems changed all of a sudden. Staff and even customers start murmuring, factions or group of staff and officers emerge and the cordial atmosphere seems to be missing distinctly. This is because of team conflict in the branch the symptoms of which may be summarized as under:

1. **Absenteeism, employees avoid coming to work deliberately.** When conflict arises in the team staff will not cooperate and will go on leave just to put the team leader in trouble. They will keep the work pending or unattended and will keep the branch head uninformed and will proceed on leave without taking prior permission or sanction of leave.

2. **Diminishing trend of mutual cooperation among staff.** When there is no cooperation among staff in day to day working it is sure there is some conflict in the workplace. In such situation when a less experienced or junior staff seeks some guidance or help from his senior he doesn't get a proper response rather he is asked to get the support from branch head.

3. **Hostile approach, growing nature of anger even on petty matters.**

4. **Employees start talking behind each other's back.**

5. **Low morale. Employees do not want to share any responsibility. Every staff wants to pit the burden of any task on other's shoulders.**

6. **Increase in complaints.** There are two types of complaints: First complaints emanating directly from customers against poor service rendered by the bank. Second, some smart disgruntled staff instigate customers to lodge complaints against bank cleverly, not disclosing their names. Local staff may play a lead role in this exercise. This generally happens in a bank when senior

award staff of the branch are given more responsibility by the branch head. Since such staff were not in the habit of sharing any higher responsibility earlier due to whatever reasons and now the branch manager is firm to get them involved in the mainstream they very often resort to such dirty practice to demotivate their team leader. Unfortunately in many such situations even the controlling office do not extend any worthwhile support to the team leader.

7. **Showing no interest in completion of allotted work by the employees taking the shield of lame excuses.** To mitigate this problem team leader must have an eye over the progress of such erring staff. If this is not done other staff may also fall in the same line to aggravate the problem for the team leader.

8. **Avoiding presence in the meetings called by the team leader.** The team leader must ensure that the information of meeting reaches all concerned well in time. When there is some conflict in the team the staff deliberately abstain from meetings quoting lame excuses.

9. **Frequent unresolved misunderstandings.** Some of the staff deliberately and knowingly create misunderstanding and do not allow any solution to come in. This tendency on their part creates conflict in the work place.

10. **In meetings putting several questions without contributing any solution or suggestion.** Those having negative and non – cooperative attitudes will just ask questions in meetings to vitiate the environment.

They don't have any solution in their mind nor they are interested in resolving any issue.

11. **Keeping team leader in dark of various developments concerning bank.** The disgruntled staff deliberately don't pass any information of importance to their team leader so that the situation becomes worse and the business leader's position becomes embarrassing before higher management. This happens when there is conflict of team in the work place.

12. **Lack of respect for the team leader.** When there is team conflict in the workplace the staff don't show any respect to their leaders rather they wish to destabilize the working atmosphere so that the position of branch head is lowered in the eyes of higher management as well as customers and the erring staff may get an opportunity to blame their leader. This way they don't show any respect to their team leader. When the team leader calls for support and co – operation they don't show any positive response and respect to such calls.

How to avoid conflict in workplace

In a bank all the staff and officers are well educated and in general have good educational and family background. Some of them also have good social reputations. They have their own conviction in any matter which is based upon some principle. It is not necessary that they are agreeable to others point of view all the time. Therefore difference of opinion among them is quite natural because each one of them has his or her own thinking on a particular issue. It is human nature to disagree and disagreements are many times beneficial when dealt with properly. Thus conflict in a workplace is not necessarily a bad thing because very often a constructive and positive conflict ensures a high performing team of workers.

It is not necessary that all workers should blindly subscribe to the view of their leader. Their opinion may be better for the bank and may not be in consonance with their leader. Here conflict arises if the team leader does not foresee it's consequences. When different view points involved in a conflict are appreciated and taken care of appropriately the conflict is automatically resolved. The conflict resolution increases understanding and respect of staff and team leader. Handling of conflict in a workplace is an art and only a mature and positive minded team leader having practical attitude can handle it successfully.

It is always advisable that the team leader must feel the signs of conflict in the branch at a very initial stage. The issues which are hidden must be addressed before it is too late. In day to day working problems may arise but the problems which are knowingly or unknowingly not addressed and kept hidden by the team leader or not brought to the knowledge of team leader by team members are likely to hit the performance of bank adversely. On the other hand good conflict in an organization always comes with new suggestions, ideas, solutions and opportunities for the team leader to enhance the ability, tact and performance. At the same time a bad conflict which is recurring in nature causes fall in productivity, performance and ultimately the morale of workforce.

The following methods may be adopted for avoiding conflicts:

1. **Team leader should be a good listener.** He should never stick to an inflexible opinion.
2. **Team leader should forget that he is right all the time.**

3. When the conflict in workplace is due to relationship between team member and team leader, it is suggested that the **team leader should take some alone time to smoothen the complexity involved in the conflict.**
4. **Discussion with teammates should be planned by the team leader.**
5. When above preparations are completed the **team leader should initiate counselling of teammates or mediation.**

The team leader should have the ability to understand the underlying reasons of workplace conflict and endeavour to avoid this:

(a) Human emotions play an important role as staff become uncomfortable and irritated in unreasonable workplace situations. This may cause stress and they may not feel happy while working. If this continues the level of stress is increased and leads to resentment. When this is not controlled the staff lacking confidence act out constantly in their attempts to prove themselves always be right. In order to avoid this the team leader has to be very realistic in his goals. Only then the conflict will be minimized.

(b) The team leader should be acceptable, positive, trustworthy and willing to cooperate his team. He should always try to find out if any of his staff is facing some genuine problem in which the leader can paly some constructive role to ameliorate the same. Once the problem is identified he should not lose any time to resolve the issue.

(c) When the situation becomes difficult to handle and the teammates are angry, it is necessary that the team leader responds compassionately by acknowledging the feelings of his teammates without any reservation. If anger is directed towards him a sincere, prompt and unconditional apology is always disarming.

(d) This is very useful advice for the team leader. He must avoid person centred statements that begin with "You never..........", "You always.........." etc. He should keep in mind not to make his teammates feel guilty or asset blame whatever past incident be. Words which incite anger should never find a place in conversation of the team leader. He should always remember that words of anger are more harmful than a polite advice to a staff though he has committed some mistake.

(e) Finally, a mediation session always works. If conflict seems inevitable to bring tension in the workplace a mediation, preferably with an impartial third party, say HR personnel or head of the controlling office is the best way to put an end to arising conflict.

Steps of conflict resolution in workplace

The resolution of conflict in workplace depends upon whether both sides are willing to end the conflict in the interest of bank. Here one side is workforce and the other is bank manager as team leader. Without resolution of conflict they cannot reach the common goal of bank. When they are having some conflict in their mind every time they would be thinking how to prove other person wrong. With this mindset they cannot think for the growth of bank. **The conflict resolution in workplace of a bank involves following steps:**

1. **Conflict analysis**
2. **Brainstorming solutions**

3. Collaborating
4. Verbal communication
5. Convening meetings
6. Creativity
7. Decision making.

Conflict Resolution Flow Chart

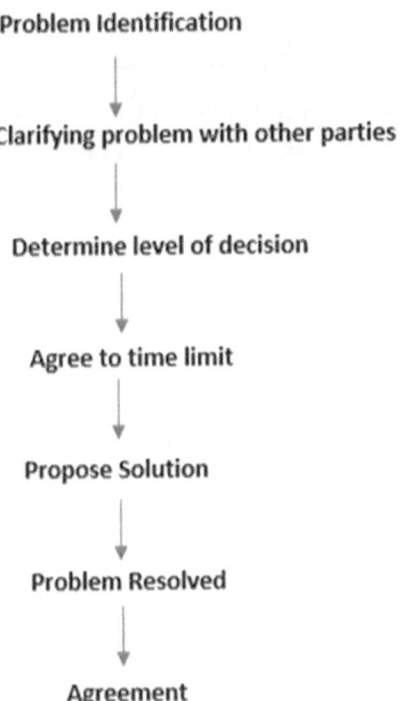

Conflict resolution strategies

Many thinkers have suggested the ways and means for resolution of workplace conflict in an organization. However, the strategies suggested by **Kenneth W. Thomas and Ralph H. Kilmann** are

widely accepted who have developed following five strategies for conflict resolution in workplace:
1. Avoiding
2. Competitive approach
3. Compromising
4. Accommodating
5. Collaborating.

1. **Avoiding** – Though conflict in an organization may be due to various reasons steps are necessitated for it's resolution in time. The method of avoiding for conflict resolution is adopted in workplace when discomfort of confrontation gradually increases the possible reward of resolution. By avoiding conflict, resolution is not achieved.

2. **Competitive approach** – The assumption of this strategy is that only one side of the resolution process wins, others lose. It is rarely a good strategy to resolve the conflict.

3. **Compromising** – When parties of conflict resolution are partially assertive and cooperative listening to each other, this strategy is adopted for resolution of conflict. In this process it is not necessary that both the parties achieve what they desire. In fact the position is quite different. Both the parties lose a bit and none of them is able to get the whole expectation.

4. **Accomodating** – In this process of conflict resolution one party gives in to the demands of other. Here the two parties are workforce on one side and the bank manager on other side in the role of team leader. Either of the two accommodates other just to keep cordial

environment. Thus they cooperate other party to accommodate. But one thing is most remarkable here. Excess accommodation leads to a situation where most assertive party commands the process and carries away the entire conversation between the two.

5. **Collaborating** – When both parties in the process of conflict resolution are assertive and cooperative, the process of collaborating is adopted by them. Here a shared solution between the two is emerged which is accepted by all.

Based upon the above, conflict resolution in a workplace may be divided broadly into following three category:

A. Win – Win
B. Win – Lose
C. Lose – Lose.

According to **Kenneth W. Thomas and Ralph H. Kilmann** theory, as narrated above the following situation may arise in conflict resolution-

A. Competing and collaborating in a win – win resolution process.
B. Accommodating is a win-lose resolution process.
C. Compromising and avoiding is a lose – lose resolution process.

For a bank manager as team leader win – win technique is always preferred.

CHAPTER 10

STRESS MANAGEMENT FOR TEAM LEADER

What is Stress?

In medical or biological context stress is defined as physical, mental or emotional reaction of a body when change occurs. Stress is a normal part of life. This can be caused by environment, own body or thoughts of a person.

So stress is body's reaction to any change that requires an adjustment. The body reacts to these changes with physical, mental or even emotional responses.

Stress causes a surge of harmones in body. When stress is detected in body a small region in the base of the brain called hypothelamus reacts by stimulating the body to produce harmones which include adrenaline and cortisol.

As a result of this a little acceleration is caused in heart and lungs and ultimately it results in violent muscular action as well. So stress is our body's reaction to a challenge or unexpected demand as perceived by us.

When it helps us to avoid danger or meet some deadline it is positive.

But when it lasts for a long time it may harm our health in various ways. When we apprehend that someone may cause us physical assault our body immediately responds automatically to escape the dangerous situation and we are saved. In medical terminology this is called ' survival stress'.

When the stress is of short duration it causes production of brain chemicals known as neurotrophins and strengthens the connection between neurons in the brain. This is the main tool to improve productivity of a man who is in an acute stress.

Scientifically good stress is called "eustress" which is primarily responsible to improve a person's performance, ability and also quality of life.

A team leader faces challenges always and many times he is not fully prepared to face the same either physically or mentally which causes some sort of stress.

Symptoms of Stress

A team leader may notice symptoms of stress when following up a chronic NPA borrower of bank and annual closing is approaching fast and the branch is lagging far behind the business targets. If he is taking all measures to recover bank' dues and borrower is not traceable or is not cooperating in such situation stress is inevitable. Even in personal life managing finances and coping with social relations may be challenging which are likely to cause stress.

For a student stress comes automatically when dates of examination are announced. So stress is everywhere. Long term stress may affect a person physically as well as mentally. In such situation it is very essential for a team leader to control stress otherwise he can't lead a normal life. This is possible only when he is aware of the symptoms of stress.

A person may experience any of the following symptoms of stress –

A. Physical symptoms
B. Emotional symptoms
C. Cognitive symptoms

A. **Physical symptoms** – Nervousness or shaking, cold or sweaty hands, diarrhea, Constipation and nausea, headaches, sexual problems, chest pain, increased heart Beat, insomnia, grinding teeth are some of the common physical symptoms of stress.

B. **Emotional symptoms** – Emotional symptoms of stress cover frustration, anger, moody behaviour, losing control over self, depression, tendency of avoiding others. A person having this kind of stress may have an irritating nature.

C. **Cognitive symptoms** – Forgetfulness, poor judgement, pessimistic thinking, racing thoughts, inability to concentrate or focus on any matter. In addition to above the behavioural symptoms include procrastinating and avoiding responsibilities, use of alcohol or drugs, use of cigarettes, tiredness, loss of appetite or even eating too much etc.

These symptoms Also cover psychological symptoms viz. anxiety, depression, anger, restlessness or loss of interest in sex etc.

Good Stress and Bad Stress

In chronic stress which continues for a longer period our body wears itself down. Depending upon level of stress it can be good or bad for our body. When we are stressed and manage them efficiently our performance is improved. When the team leader is going to attend a review meeting at a short notice he may feel stressed but prepare for the same.

For this, preparation of ppt, slides, notes, collection of performance figures vis-a-vis targets, strategies to fill the gap between performance and targets are taken meticulously. This gives the team leader enough energy and confidence to complete the task so that the review meeting becomes meaningful.

On the contrary when the stress is heavy and continues for a longer period without any visible sign of redressal it may drain the energy which affects efficiency at work adversely.

For example when the team leader does not get performing, skilled or experienced team of staff and even there is no encouraging positive response from higher management the team leader continues to remain in stress. This decreases his efficiency because he does not get any support and motivation. When a person is in acute stress support and motivation are very necessary to cope with the difficult situation. Having too much of work to do or even having internal problems with team members are sufficient reasons to cause stress to the team leader.

This may lead to illness, increased blood pressure or even heart disease. A stress which decreases efficiency is bad stress. Because of bad stress cortisol level in body increases and it affects learning and memory power adversely. The tendency of forgetting things increases in the person. This is likely to lower the immunity also of the person who is facing this type of problem. Ultimately it increases blood pressure, cholesterol and becomes some cause of heart disease.

Thus stress is inevitable in our normal day to day life. Since it is natural we can't have any escape from this. While good stress motivates us to perform bad stress affects our body and mind both physically and psychologically. In order to perform team leader must learn the art of stress management so that the effect of stress on body and mind can be reduced to a bearable level. Some of the methods to reduce bad stress for team leader are listed below –

1. **Accept the events which are not under your control.** If you ignore this you will only waste your time and energy and the result will be harmful.
2. **Have a positive attitude and thoughts.** If you are of pessimistic mind you cannot find any happiness and will see everything with suspicious approach. This will not help you in reducing bad stress.
3. **Set an achievable goal for yourself.** Never be crazy for unrealistic targets. If you are always thinking that "only sky is the limit" without looking into the reality you may soon get disappointed over your failure. This will only increase bad stress.
4. **Don't get scared of your failures and never dwell on disappointment.**
5. **Avoid anger, defensive and passive attitude.**
6. **Take balanced food rich in fibres and nutrition.** Take fresh vegetables and seasonal fruits in your daily diet.
7. **Do regular exercise. Practice meditation, yoga** and deep abdominal breathing exercise daily.
8. **Spare some time for your hobbies and develop them.** Spend time in walking in nearby park
9. **Learn the art of time management.** This will keep you happy and positive feelings will come in your mind automatically.
10. **Be happy and take sound sleep.**
11. **Never take alcohol or medicines to combat stress.** In case of acute stress take help of psychologist.

The 4 A's of Stress Management

Sometimes the stress level is so high that the business leader finds it very difficult to cope with. Shortage of staff, unrealistic and non achievable business targets given by higher management, hostile attitude of customers etc. may be the reasons. In such situation it is advisable to either reduce the stressors or enhance the ability to cope or both. To deal with this it is necessary to have sound sleep preferably 6 – 8 hours, regular physical exercise, positive thinking, proper nutritious diet are usually recommended. Before going to bed at least half an hour break from revision is suggested. Morning walk preferably brisk walk, depending upon health of 30 – 45 minutes or regular physical exercise uses up the harmones and nervous energy produced due to excessive stress and also keeps the body fit and mind cheerful. Exercise relaxes the muscles and flow of blood around the body is increased. Pessimistic outlook does not help rather it increases the level of stress. Hence the outlook must be positive.

In addition to above the bank manager as a business leader or team leader has to master the following four strategies popularly known as "4 A's" to cope with the stress:

    a. Avoid
    b. Alter
    c. Accept
    d. Adapt

a. **Avoid** – Stress can be avoided to reap the benefits of a lighter load in following ways –
    1. Control your surroundings.
    2. Avoid people who bother you.

3. Learn to say 'No'.
4. List your tasks priority wise.

b. **Alter** – During times of stress take inventory and then attempt to change the situation for better.
   1. Respectfully ask others to change their behaviour.
   2. Communicate your inner feelings openly.
   3. Manage your time judiciously.
   4. State limits in advance.

c. **Accept** – When you don't have any option except to accept, your strategies will be
   1. Talk with someone.
   2. Forgive.
   3. Practice positive self talk.
   4. Learn from your mistakes.

d. **Adapt** – Thinking you can't cope is one of the greatest stressors. That's why adapting is the most helpful in dealing with stress.
   1. Practice thought stopping.
   2. Reframe the issue.
   3. Adopt a "mantra".
   4. Create an asset column. Look at the big picture.

Self care methods to deal with stress

According to **Elizabeth Scott** a multifaceted process of the purposeful engagement in activities promoting both physical and mental good health is required as self care method to deal with stress by a business leader or bank manager as a team leader.

Five types of most popular self care practices are:
a. **Physical self care**
b. **Social self care**
c. **Mental self care**
d. **Spiritual self care**
e. **Emotional self care.**

However these self care strategies vary from man to man i.e. Self care is not a ' one size fits all ' strategy. A housewife who is most of the time busy in household works may need social self care as well as physical self care. She takes care the whole family but very often her own physical well being is badly neglected. At the same time she may not get enough time to make good relationship in social circles which is also required. So she needs social self care.

a. Physical Self Care

It is an old saying that a good mind remains with a good body. So a team leader must maintain good health to keep his mind free from all kinds of worries or mental stress. This can be had by doing physical activities, doing regular exercise, taking medication if advised by doctor, having sound and adequate sleep, balanced and nutritious diet, walking etc. maintaining cleanness, good hygiene, healthy life style also come under this category.

b. Social Self Care

A team leader cannot live aloof from society, if he wishes to be free from stress. He must manage time to make friends, take part in social activities and gathering, get recognition of his talent and knowledge in the society. Taking part in social recreations, social groups viz. Rotary Club, Lions Club, Resident Welfare

Association etc. may help the team leader in eliminating stress to a great extent.

c. Mental Self Care

The team leader should plan for keeping himself busy with activities of his choice. If he has any liking for gardening, writing or singing, painting he must spare some time for promoting such hobbies. These activities keep him mentally healthy and satisfied and will thus eliminate some of his stress.

d. Spiritual Self Care

When we take any action to deepen our connection with our higher self, this is called spiritual self care. The most popular spiritual self care is meditation. Practising gratitude is another form of spiritual self care in which one focuses on positive meditative things. Spending some time in nature forgetting wordly problems or participating in religious service gives a team leader a sense of community, reinforces the values and beliefs and connects them with something greater than themselves.

A team leader must not ignore his liking for a spiritual or religious life style if he likes them. Meditation, taking part in religious service prayer and other practices will certainly help him in decreasing his stress to a good extent. By doing meditation on regular basis a person's life becomes more manageable. After meditating one feels refreshed and is able to keep away from worries, anxiety and concerns.

e. Emotional Self Care

Emotions of a person play very important role in increasing or decreasing stress from time to time. While anger, anxiety, fear and feeling of loneliness contribute significantly to increase stress, if these are taken care strategically a team leader may eliminate stress arising due to this. Team leader must develop ways and means to process and keep his emotions under control. Anger of a person can be eliminated by finding it's root cause and taking remedial steps. For removing the fear of loneliness it is suggested that team leader must involve his teammates in arriving some decisions.

Time management strategies to eliminate stress

In the present age driven by technology team leaders are always accessible through emails, mobile phones or video conferences. Place and time are no barriers in connecting team leaders. This is helpful in increasingly productivity and reducing customer complaints but at the same time it also increases stress. Due to this ever increasing stress team leaders are suffering and are living in the state of depression. Very often finding no way to eliminate stress some of them also commit suicide. This is a very dangerous situation and we are required to deal with this matter with all seriousness it deserves.

While meditation and yoga exercise regularly can help in mitigating the stress that is not enough. According to a survey conducted by the American Institute of Stress, 40% of workers reported their job very or extremely stressful. Taking a walk around the office during lunch hour is not sufficient to reduce the level of stress. Hence to solve this problem when self care is no ultimate solution team leaders are suggested to adopt following practices:

A. Delegate Tasks.
B. Take a Clarity Break.
C. Learn to say No.

A. Delegate Tasks

For every team leader, demands whether at home or at workplace, never stop rather increase all the time. In such situation team leader is puzzled as he is not in a position to do justice to all such demands. Everybody has his/her own limitations. If the demands are ever increasing it is not possible for anybody to fulfil the same.

The best way to do this is to delegate the task among fellow workers. This will save time and stress will be reduced considerably. In the very beginning it appears to be difficult to delegate but you will often find that the tasks you don't like are what someone enjoys. If you are strong in analytics you will prefer analysis of performance figures but those who like field visits will seldom like this. **Baird Brightman** shares valuable insight on delegating. "Define the 'what' and delegate the 'how'." Team leader should give the responsibility for accomplishing task to others and let them to sort out the best way to go about accomplishing it.

B. Take a Clarity Break

Clarity break means one practices regularly to get away from the workload of office, turn off all devices including phone calls and distractions and allow one time to sit calmly and think. Essentially it is an unstructured commitment to clear one's head. In this process the person does not go through emails, does not respond them, does not read circulars or messages or follow up on given tasks. The team leader is supposed to find answers to some questions viz. is he focusing on right things, is he true to his commitment, are his strategies going on well; if the answer is negative has he any back up plan?

For a bank manager as team leader the clarity break practice is very much essential and helpful as it gives an opportunity to explore the actions of team leader are as per original plan of action and if required what steps are to be taken to redirect the actions to achieve the goal.

C. Learn to say "No"

A team leader must know the value of time. He is supposed to be ruthless with his time. He must develop the courage to say ' No '. Having courage to say ' No' to the little things in life gives him the power and willingness to say ' Yes' to big things of importance. It is not necessary to respond to every call when you are busy with some important work. There is no point in allowing all to come in when you require a few hours to work on big case say appraisal of a big project. Or you may be busy in preparation of next review meeting papers. This way your concentration will show amazing result which you cannot imagine. If you are managing your time this way you will be able to manage stress effectively.

Many commitments mean more stress. Generally people want to be helpful and don't want to pass up an opportunity that may forward them personally or professionally. When someone asks you to take on a new responsibility or job, don't be too quick to say 'Yes'. Instead tell them you will think about it and need to check your schedule. List out all the additional tasks you would be saying 'Yes' to by committing and evaluate if this is aligned with your greater goals. If it is not say 'No'.

CHAPTER 11

THE ART OF POSITIVE CRITICISM

While reviewing the performance of an employee in workplace if it is found that the output of the employee is far below expectation to meet organisation's pre set goals, it is necessary on the part of team leader to make the employee aware of this fact tactfully so as to make him realise his shortcomings and improve the performance. For a bank manager as team leader motivating the employee, who is a poor or average performer, through positive reinforcement is not as challenging as criticising or taking some disciplinary action.

The criticism has many results but one cannot afford it to be counter productive. This art of employee's criticism is called positive criticism. For a team leader criticism of an employee from whom he gets the work done for the bank criticism is like a challenge. The team leader is expected to have a courage to make his subordinate aware of the shortcomings in work performance.

Secondly the team leader has to prepare himself to face the defensive and spontaneous emotional reaction of the employee. So criticising an employee over his/her poor or substandard performance is not an easy job but it is a big challenge for the team leader. To handle this situation one has to learn the art of positive criticism so that the criticism is constructive and not counter productive.

Banks have the system of periodical performance review meetings in which threadbare discussion on performance of branch vis-a-vis targets allotted take place.

For a team leader too such performance evaluation discussion with the team member should be arranged to share the corrective input. To make the meeting more fruitful following preparations require to be done before hand by the team leader:
1. Written instructions to the employee should be kept in hand with all necessary relevant documentation.
2. The deficiency or shortcoming in the work performance of the employee should be shown to him along with the list of tasks given to him in the beginning of review period.
3. Prepare a list of your suggestions you wish to get implemented by the employee to meet the allotted target.
4. Team leader must avoid admonishing the employee instead he should have a positive and helpful outlook.
5. After the discussion takes place a mutually agreed set of action points should be prepared and shared. As far as possible a definite timeline should be set with consent of the employee.

Sometimes high work pressure, time constraints and other, genuine factors all play together to subdue the performance level of the employee causing a big gap between targets and achievement. Generally these are the external factors which are unforeseen in the beginning but come in the way of working later on. The employee and team leader have no control over them. All these factors must be in the mind of team leader at the time of performance review of an employee. The ultimate objective of the team leader in such a situation should be to improve the skills and efficiency of the employee and not to admonish or discourage him. He should have control over self under stress which is also known as emotional intelligence skill.

To tackle the above situation **"Sandwich Technique"** of artful criticism is adopted. Here the team leader diplomatically and tactfully makes his employee aware of his shortcomings in performance without hurting his sentiments. This method is very popular and is also known as **"Feedback Sandwich"** technique. In fact this is a constructive criticism which aims to impart something through a valid, reasonable and acceptable opinion. Since it doesn't close the door of conversation it is positive in nature. In this method:

1. **The opening of discussion is always positive.**
2. **Criticism and corrective feedback is then shared with the employee.**
3. **The interaction ends with a positive statement. The statement blends the initial positive opening statement with an expression of confidence that performance will be corrected as discussed.**

Here one point is very remarkable. By starting positive you show that you are on the side of employee who is being criticised. That means you are interested not only in criticising the employee but you are with the employee as you understand the things in true manner. Again when you end your conversation with positive statement the employee feels that you are really interested in his improvement and hence he doesn't feel emotionally hurt.

Case Example

We give below a case example of the Branch Head to whom the credit officer has put up a credit proposal for review and when the Branch Head goes through it he finds several mistakes in the proposal. Now before speaking to the credit officer the

Branch Head may adopt the Sandwich Technique by sending the following note to the credit officer:

This was a big proposal involving many critical issues of bank finance which we are required to take care. You have nicely covered all these aspects which shows that you have a good idea of the prospective borrower and have a firm grip over this proposal.

I would like to know how this review proposal was prepared which contains many mistakes in calculation of financial ratios which carry much importance for review of a credit proposal. Let me know who assisted you in preparing CMA data and how much time was taken in giving the review proposal a final shape. The Due Diligence Certificate is also missing.

After this the Branch Head must have a thorough discussion with the credit officer highlighting the main issues of concern in the proposal and how to rectify the irregularities. After that he should share the following:

Our discussion was very helpful. Your suggestion to include the performance of other similar units in the area is really appreciable. Let us collect the data from lead bank manager and also rectify the mistakes in the proposal. Please attach the Due Diligence Certificate as per bank's prescribed format.

The team leader should always try this Sandwich Technique every time he is not satisfied with the performance of his employee and want to get things done differently.

# CHAPTER 12

BANKING INDUSTRY AT THE DIGITAL AGE

Modern banking has grown by leaps and bound and now it is all about anytime, anywhere banking based upon a robust, innovative, secure and fool proof digital infrastructure. Today the customers are tech savvy and to meet their demands of secure products and services the banking area is undergoing a major transformation. 'Banking at your convenience' has become the main mantra and implementation of new technology has disrupted the banking based on traditional methods and practices significantly.

In this context now digitalization in banks has become the new differentiator for meeting the future requirement of customers. Banking industry, one of the oldest industries of the world has grown immensely by continuously adapting to new changes as per requirement of customers and new innovations in technology. With the introduction of digitalization innovations in banking have taken up very rapidly and now banking is no more just a business transaction. It has penetrated deep into the lives of people, be it rural banking, FOREX trading or social banking. Banks are now using data by way of personalized relationship.

The competition among bankers in this field is so fierce that banks are now deploying their services to customers, using latest technology in purely customer centric manner. In the present situation technology is undisputed gateway for a desired customer experience of utmost satisfaction.

Banks are now innovating and experimenting using latest technology for their business operations and making relationship with the customer robust so that they may easily ensure their firm and solid position among the competitors in the banking industry.

For the bankers digitalization is now not a new thing. New innovations by banks in the field of digitalization comes with new challenges and problems which a team leader has to face with all preparedness, adopt the above technology successfully, implement the same and solve the problems arising out of this. They have to keep themselves abreast of latest technological advancement which is useful for bank and it's customers.

They have to keep their eyes open on other sectors of financial market also. Business leaders have to address all queries of customers in view of their changing behaviour concerning banking by using latest technology.

The adoption of new advanced technology, impact of fierce competition among the peers and rapid increase of highly demanding customers have made a drastic change in banking service which is clearly visible now. Therefore team leaders are now have to adopt a new strategy and new approach to procure the business from market. Earlier customers used to come to bank ask for what they wanted and bankers used to satisfy them by fulfilling their demands. Now this has completely changed. In present day most progressive financial services cultures, bankers are approaching prospective customers, explaining to them different kinds of products and services of the bank. Thus the shift from the previous scenario of banking service is quite visible now.

Even then this is not sufficient in the present day advanced technology age. So banking has been affected accordingly. With this change due to new technology, customers have easy access to networking/social networking sites which provide them the opportunity to experience with the bank and bankers nowadays are required not to have the knowledge of all products and services only but they have to develop their skill to understand the needs of the customers critically, take decision promptly and go into action without any loss of time. It is not necessary that everything as written in bank's book of instructions/manual are to be followed literally, rather to meet the customer's expectations. For this team leaders have been granted enhanced discretionary powers by their higher administrative offices.

So in today's context team leaders cannot just follow the written instructions of their superior authority but they have to modify and adjust their strategies to meet both customers' expectations and Bank's policy guidelines. They cannot go beyond the framework of bank's directives but have to be flexible in their approach, adopt the latest technology in making quick decisions by adopting digitalization wherever necessary. By adopting digitalization

1. Banks can provide enhanced customer service of superior quality.
2. Human error will be reduced to build the customer loyalty.
3. Cashless transactions can take place.
4. Efficiency and productivity will increase by reducing costs.

5. Both through the alignment of goals and the opening of new communication channels the digitalization of business improves internal communication.
6. Healthy marketing competition are well maintained.

The effect of COVID – 19 on digital transformation in the workplace

The global lockdown caused by COVID – 19 pandemic has noticeable impacts on our personal and professional lives in many ways. The banking business world is no exception to this. Hence bank business leaders have now no choice but to review their strategies to face the new crisis caused by the pandemic.

Now the business leaders or bank managers as team leaders have adopted the digital transformation initiatives. This is very challenging no doubt. This is a wake up call for business leaders to adopt in practice digital transformation. Before COVID – 19 around 70% of business companies had a digital transformation or were working on one. Now COVID – 19 has compelled them to accelerate their digital transformation initiatives. The following are the reasons for this :

1. Due to continuous lockdown for a fairly long period, implementation of social distancing etc. employees are physically separated. As a result of this the way they collaborate and work as a team has got a drastic change. Due to quarantines, restrictions on travel and movement, closures of educational institutions viz. schools, colleges etc. partial opening of shops, sick family members have a direct impact on business. Many companies are of the view that technology can help them in current difficult situations. That's why we are

now witnessing many digital transformation projects and their implementation.

2. In current period of COVID – 19 it is necessary to have our internal communication clear, unambiguous and transparent. For users it must be easy to comprehend. So improving internal communication is the most important digital transformation project for most of the business houses. This will ensure right inflow of information at all level.

3. During COVID – 19 outbreak the priority of the companies are to protect their employees and help reduce the spread of virus. Work from home have been allowed to maintain the productivity. They are also in search for marketing, sales and other essential activities to ensure continuous business performance that affect productivity.

4. In order to ensure future growth of business, team leaders are required to show and put in practice their leadership skills. For this they are getting necessary support from new digital transformation and technology initiatives.

Chapter 13

SWOT ANALYSIS

SWOT is an acronym of Strength, Weakness, Opportunity and Threat. SWOT analysis is a technique first developed by **Albert Humphrey,** American business and management consultant in the year 1960s for analysing organisations' financial data of 500 largest corporations which occupied place in the prestigious world famous magazine Fortune. Since then various companies are utilizing this technique as a useful tool to formulate their strategies and road map for growth and performance.

Strength refers to a core competency of the business where it has a competitive advantage when it comes to a customer value propositions. Further these strengths can be either tangible or intangible. Tangible strengths are those which can be clearly identified, measured or realized. On the other hand intangible strengths cannot be physically touched or physically measured. Similarly opportunity is an environmental condition in macro or industry environment that can improve organization's position relative to that of competitors. A threat is a forecasted environmental condition that is not in control and possesses the potential to harm the business.

Purpose of SWOT analysis

SWOT analysis is widely used to study the internal and external determinants affecting the growth and performance of an organization. These determinants have their direct bearing on the well being of the organization. These are : Strength (internal), Weakness (internal), Opportunity (external) and Threat (external). By identifying these internal and external environments of the organization these factors are further analysed which influence functioning and performance of the organization. Once this analysis is done, based upon strategic planning method future course of action is formulated to improve the overall performance.

The analysis of external environmental factors is commonly divided into macro environmental factors and micro environmental factors. Macro environmental factors include demographic, political, technical and economic factors. Micro environmental factors consist of suppliers, partners, workforce, quality of product and services, customers etc. Once strategies are prepared based upon SWOT analysis these contributing factors are closely monitored and functioning , efficiency, productivity etc. are improved as desired. Thus the SWOT analysis helps in understanding the immediate causes of success and failures of the organization in competing the competitors in the market. Through this technique strategies are drawn up to improve the performance.

Objectives of SWOT analysis

1. To identify the main economic and environmental factors of a company to plan for strategic action plan for achieving corporate objectives.

2. The identification followed by detailed analysis of internal environmental factors viz. weaknesses and threats help to prepare strategic action points to mitigate potential risks and other problems of the organization. The internal environmental factors viz. strengths. and

opportunities focus on core of business by eliminating deficiencies or sub standard performance.

3. By doing SWOT analysis one can easily determine the health of the company. The positive points namely strength and opportunity can be strengthened to improve the performance of organization. At the same time diminishing the negative factors namely weakness and threat, one can improve the functioning of organization.

SWOT diagram

A SWOT diagram analyses a business entity by focussing on each of the following contributing factors viz. strength, weakness, opportunity and threat.

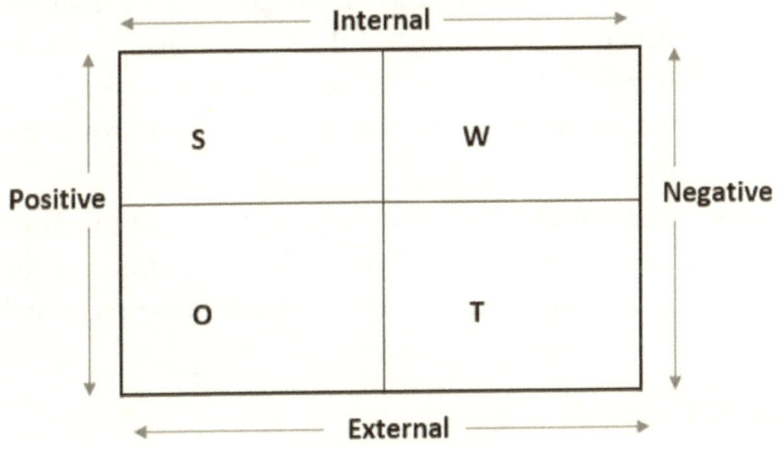

(Swot Diagram)

1. A SWOT diagram should be specific and to the point. Only relevant points should find place in this diagram. In the four blocks shown above in the diagram all factors belonging to strength, weakness, opportunity

and threat should be written which have true relevance to the performance of the organisation in actual sense. However they should be brief as far as possible. Information irrelevant to the performance of business entity should not be taken in this diagram.

2. Before drawing the SWOT diagram it is necessary to get right feedback from employees, customers and others who have an interest in the growth, reputation and well being of the organization. In this manner the position of organization can be had from varied angles which have a direct bearing on its performance, growth and market reputation.

3. While preparing the SWOT diagram it is necessary to keep aim and objective of the organization in mind otherwise the true analysis may get diverted from the main issue. For example if the SWOT diagram is being prepared for SME loan factory of bank we have to keep this in our mind and complete the diagram from this angle.

4. Once SWOT diagram is prepared it should be updated on regular intervals otherwise the true position of the organization cannot be obtained and the strategies and action points will be faulty.

SWOT analysis of a bank

Some of the important environmental factors of SWOT analysis of a bank may be summarized as under :

1. **Strength:**
    a. Availability of professional, dedicated, experienced and well trained manpower.

b. Efficiency is maintained at the highest level.
c. Strong financials. Full control over fresh slippages, NPAs etc. Regular follow up of potential NPA accounts.
d. Compliance of capital adequacy and prudential norms as prescribed by Reserve Bank of India.
e. Fully computerised, TBM branches and techno savvy staff.
f. High service quality rendered by staff.
g. Robust financial reserves.
h. Broader product range.
I. Attractive ambience. Convenient layout of service outlets.
j. Convenient positioning. Easy approach.
k. Very strong Corporate Social Responsibility (CSR).

2. **Weakness:**
   a. Mixed quality staff. Shortage of trained staff in the field of banking where customers' demand is more.
   b. Very limited online advertising experience.
   c. Pricing of product as per market trend. This affects cost of product and services being offered to customers.
   d. After merger of different banks both old and new branches are operating in the same area of operation.
   f. Although highly networked number of branches is limited.
   g. Dissimilarity exits between old and new branches due to their varying work culture and image.
   h. Poor knowledge and lack of adequate training among many staff of the merged banks.

3. **Opportunity:**
   a. Availability of data on most of the financial parameters gives a leverage.
   b. Relationship can be strengthened with well wishers, influencers and government departments.
   c. Service products can be differentiated based upon their costs vis-a-vis utility.
   d. Due to good image of the bank customer relationship can be enhanced.
   f. By opening new branches in the command area further business can be procured.
   g. Service and products can be advertised online to lure more and more customers in bank's fold.
   h. As per demand of customers product mix can be expanded.
   i. Through customer focused approach the outlook can be made customer centric which will be beneficial for the bank.

4. **Threat:**
   a. Fixed cost on rising trend.
   b. Customers becoming more conscious and sensitive towards increasing costs.
   c. Difficulty in increasing customer base of good networth. High networth customers are not willing to switch over from other banks.
   d. Arrival of new competitors causing shrinkage of our market share.
   e. Intermittent technological faults causing inconvenience to staff and customer unrest.

f. Rapid increase in number of frauds committed online over which branch has no direct control.

g. The unpredictable market condition.

h. Ever increasing cost of maintaining large data base for the purpose of monitoring.

Personal SWOT analysis of a Business Leader

Personal SWOT analysis of a business leader is a unique way to organize, prioritize and plan his/her personal development. The simplistic format of SWOT diagram is nothing but an in – depth analysis which maybe required to improve the personality of business leader as a team leader.

It is very difficult to know one's strengths and weaknesses. Therefore the help of a colleague can be taken to complete this task. When the SWOT diagram is completed by covering the views of others the result is useful and can be utilised for further improvement. A personal SWOT analysis is similar to one for business except that the business leader focusses on himself and his goals.

Before completing the SWOT diagram the team leader is required to do his self assessment for which the following questions need to be asked to himself and the answers to these questions are required to be given in an honest manner.

1. **Strength :**
   1. Prepare a list of all your strengths.
   2. Are your network of connections to people of different segment strong? If yes how strong they are.
   3. In what way you are different and unique from others ?
   4. Have you developed any skill which is useful to you in discharge of your responsibility?

5. What are your inherent talents? How can you use them for the benefit of your Organization?
6. What do other people see as your strengths?

Look at your strengths and ask yourself if they can open up any opportunity.

2. **Weakness :** Find out the areas of your weakness where you have to improve.
   1. What are your negative work habits?
   2. What would other people see as your weaknesses?
   3. Is any further improvement required in your education or training?
   4. What are you afraid to do or most likely to avoid?
   5. Do you need any special training which is required for your job role?

   Look at your weaknesses and ask yourself if you could open up opportunities by eliminating these weaknesses.

3. **Opportunity :** Look at the external factors to pursue further your goals, ambitions and dreams.
   1. Is there new demand for a skill or trait that you possess?
   2. Is there your need in the company that no one is filling?
   3. Is there any new technology in your industry for which you possess necessary qualification and previous experience?
   4. Is your company on a growth trajectory?

4. **Threat :**
   1. Is there stiff competition in your area of operation?
   2. Is there any external threat to your goal? If yes identify it.

3. Is your organization contracting from business point of view?
4. Is your organization shifting direction from its vision?
5. Is the government policy not favourable to your organization?
6. Are there any new professional standards you do not possess?
7. Are there any certification requirement that will impede your progress?

Chapter 14

SUCCESS STORY FROM Ms. LAKSHMI ANAND,

CHIEF MANAGER, BANK OF BARODA,
THILLAI NAGAR BRANCH, TRICHY, INDIA.

Sooner after my promotion to Scale – IV, I was transferred from Tooting Branch to Aldgate Branch, London; again as Branch Head. Aldgate was a bigger Branch maintaining accounts of big shots like Hinduja Group. Among NPA accounts, one account called "Barking Arms" was a big account with an outstanding amount of £780, 000 approx. (including it's proprietor 's account) and rest small accounts only. I thought of attacking this big account first. But suddenly this thought came up, it's not India, it's London, how to approach an NPA borrower. I was not much aware about the recovery process or how the people respond when we contact them for recovery. I was petty apprehensive. (To add here, in my previous Branch, Tooting, there was only one NPA account with a small amount £1000, it was a personal loan. When I called the borrower she said, "it's my office time, you can't call me now". I called her again at 7 PM, her husband picked up the phone and shouted, "don't you know, you cannot call customers after 6 to their mobile number?") So that was my experience on recovery in London.

Now this borrower was not picking up my calls. So I had to go and meet him in his business place. And it was a bar restaurant in London city itself. I had never been to a bar before so I was wandering how would the ambience be, is it proper to go there etc. Keeping my apprehensions aside, I took my credit officer, who's a local staff, along with me and boarded train from Aldgate tube station. We went inside the restaurant and met the borrower there. He was polite and said the income from restaurant is meagre and there is no way he can repay unless the restaurant is sold. He said he is making arrangements for selling the restaurant. I came back and went through his file and found that he is related to one of our local staff there. I rang him up and the staff also said he's in trouble as the business is not going well. I tried to give some pressure to the borrower through his relative.

After two weeks I called up the borrower again and asked about the status of sale arrangements. He said his solicitor is taking care of that. I took his solicitor details and contacted him. Every three days I called his solicitor who really got fed up of me and one day he said they got a buyer and sale will happen soon. Again no news for another three weeks. I went to meet the borrower again and took the contact details of the prospective buyer and buyer's solicitor. I contacted the solicitor who said they are waiting for the loan to be sanctioned for the buyer to complete the sale transaction. I asked him the details of Bank where the loan is getting processed. They said it's a high street bank but they wouldn't entertain me if contact them to know the status of loan. They insisted the borrower's solicitor to give a letter mentioning the sale amount and the proposed date of sale and that the amount will be credited directly to the loan account with us. And the solicitor obliged. Two days before the said date, I followed up and confirmed again that sale is going to take place. And finally after three months' vigorous follow up, we received the full amount. No write off, no waiver.

BOOK REVIEW

From: Dr. Ganpat Rai, Ex Principal, MPN College, Mullana (Haryana)

In this book the author has thrown light on the modern concepts of banking management and the role of bank managers as leader of their team for achieving the desired target. His contention is that as a team leader the bank manager should act as a torch bearer and light house for his team.

The long expertise and experience of the manager acts as a guide to the budding bank trainees to achieve the desired goal successfully. In fact this book is path braking for the modern banking management system and deviates from the stereotype methods adopted earlier in banking management. I am sure the new recruits and others in the industry will definitely gain much by following the methods shown by the author. Mr. Anuj Sinha, the author of the book, himself has a rich and varied experience of banking management so it is good that he has transferred his illumination knowledge of banking industry to the younger trainees for better results through this book.

The manager should only act as a first among equals in his team. The feeling of comradeship will enthuse the younger generation of trainees. In short this book is store house of modern methods of banking management techniques.

BOOK REVIEW

From: Mr. Satish C. Ahuja
      Retd. General Manager (Insp. & Audit)
      Bank of Baroda, Central Office, Mumbai.

I have gone through the book "Bank Manager as Team Leader" written by Mr. Anuj Sinha whom I know personally since 1997, when we worked together in Patna for around 2 years. He has made the best possible use of his retirement pastime by writing this book for benefit of in service officers, who hesitate to shoulder the responsibility to run the branches as Branch Head in the present days.

He has frankly spelt out that Branch Manager has to manage the bank's business by motivating his team.

Mr. Sinha has emphasized the role of Branch Manager in the present banking climate which also include to motivate the staff, working with him and to train them to handle various new developments in the banking arena particularly in digital banking for making it as customer centric. Handling various other financial products is another area where Branch Manager has to motivate his team at the Branch level.

His suggestion to use the traditional method of 4 Cs (Common goal, Cooperation, Communication & Collaboration) in order to motivate and manage his team at the Branch, is very practical approach to run the Branch.

Presently a lot of officers shirk to take the responsibility to work as Branch Manager, basic reason for this is shortage of experienced staff on one side and increase in various financial products on the other side. These twin problems reduce the output of the Branch and increase the stress on Branch Manager and his team.

So there is need to motivate and train the branch team for handling the customers' expectations.

I am sure this book will help the in service bank officers particularly Branch Head to handle their job more efficiently and without much of stress.

With good wishes.

BOOK REVIEW

From: Mr. Mukesh Sharma.
Ex Corporate General Manager
Bank of Baroda, Mumbai.

A meaningful manuscript "Bank Manager as Team Leader" is a critical analysis of the present day banking scenario viz – a – viz challenges of a Bank Manager as a Team Leader. Author Mr. Anuj Sinha coherently examines the reasons for the fear of psychosis among the young leaders in the banking industry to occupy the leadership positions beside the remedial measures to overcome that. The book is a purposeful attempt which lucidly discusses the "Customer Focused Leadership" in detail. A must read for bankers in Middle as well as Senior Management cadres.

BOOK REVIEW

From: Mr. V. C. Parmar,
Chief Manager (HRM), Bank of Baroda,
Head Office Vadodara.

Mr. Anuj Sinha having worked for Bank of Baroda, a leading Bank of the country in various capacities over three decades has beautifully written this book "Bank Manager as Team Leader" to cover the latest concepts of banking professional management which will help the bank managers to prepare them to emerge as true business leaders. How to develop leadership talent and the topics "Workplace Conflict Management" and "Stress Management for Team Leaders" will instil good sense of confidence in bank officers to share the higher responsibility to succeed as Team Leaders, which is the present day requirement of any bank. The book contains practical and easy to implement techniques and strategies written in a very simple manner which are easy to comprehend.

I have observed many good officers fear to take the lead role of branch heads due to pre conceived apprehensions of failure. This book is an essential read for them.

www.ingramcontent.com/pod-product-compliance
Lightning Source LLC
Chambersburg PA
CBHW021543200526
45163CB00015B/1160